D1548087

Written by Whitney Love

Edited by Reilly O'Neal

Cover design and layout by Rosi Germanova

Cover photo, recipe photos, and food styling by Linn Heidi Knutsen

Tableware provided by Figgjo Norway

www.figgjo.com

Published by Digital Word Norway

www.digitalword.no

First Publication February 2014

Second Publication November 2014

For more recipes and information, visit thanksforthefood.com.

Thanks *for the* Food

The Culinary Adventures of an American in Norway

By Whitney Love

Norwegian cuisine focuses on high-quality ingredients. Homemade brown gravy (page 66) is a family favorite and staple in most homes.

Contents

The church in Røros, Norway, is the fifth-largest church in the country and holds the second-oldest church organ in Norway.

Acknowledgements

This cookbook would not have been possible without the love and support of my friends and family. They come from all corners of the globe and have enriched my life—and kitchen—with their stories and recipes.

To my beloved and darling Øyvind: Thank you for showing me Norway with a new set of eyes and helping me to fall in love all over again with your home country. I am forever indebted to you for the kindness and faith you have shown me, your generous spirit, and your unwavering loyalty. Without you, this project would have remained an idea.

Preface

Thank you for reading this cookbook! It is the result of many passionate hours in the kitchen and reflects my experience as a home cook in Norway over the last seven years.

My name is Whitney, and I am an American who has been living and working in Norway since 2007. I have fallen in love with both the Norwegian way of life and the cuisine of my adopted country. I fell so hard for Norwegian cuisine that in 2009, I started a blog—*Thanks For the Food: A Norwegian Food Blog*—to document my culinary adventures.

I do my very best to:

- Eat as healthfully as I can every day, which mostly means lots of vegetables, some meat, chicken and fish, plus healthy fats—mostly from plant sources.

- Eat organic food as far as I can afford, and enjoy the occasional slice of cake (which is, of course, good for mental health).

- Ensure my plate is as varied and mixed as possible—and all the while as tasty as it can be.

Accomplishing this without going broke in Norway is a challenge that I enjoy taking on at every meal.

A collection of basic cooking utensils from Ærverdige Skottgården's history as a farm.

You will quickly learn that I love cooking, I love food, and I love Norway. So, my intention for what follows is, quite simply, to get you closer to Norway through the Norwegian recipes that I enjoy.

In addition to enjoying the recipes, you can use this book to learn more about Norway and the modern-day Norwegian way of life. I will share a bit about using the metric system, where to buy certain essential but hard-to-find ingredients, and my personal insights about life in Norway.

The food photography in this cookbook features various pieces, some manufactured over 40 years ago, from the award-winning Figgjo porcelain company. Based in the town of Figgjo, Norway, just outside of Stavanger, Figgjo has been in operation since 1941 and focuses on high-quality porcelain with modern design and traditional motifs. Thanks to their attention to quality, Figgjo has become a well-respected and well-recognized Norwegian brand. Figgjo products are used in homes and restaurants the world over and will be available for sale online in the U.S. starting in autumn 2014. More information about Figgjo can be found online at figgjo.com.

Should you have questions about an aspect of cooking (or eating) in Norway that is not mentioned here, or about Norway in general, please feel free to contact me via my blog, thanksforthefood.com.

Røros Church as seen through the window of a house inside the UNESCO World Heritage site.

Norway at a Glance

Norway is located in northern Europe, between Sweden and the North Sea. As of January 2013, the population had reached five million inhabitants.

The country is known the world over for its fjords, rugged terrain, and unspoiled natural landscape. Its capital is Oslo, with Bergen, Trondheim, and Stavanger rounding out the four largest cities in the country.

Norwegian is the official written and spoken language of Norway. It exists in two different forms: *bokmål* and *nynorsk*. Although these are in fact two different languages, *bokmål* is the form most often used in official documents, spoken on television, and taught to immigrants as a foreign language. Both language forms have several related but phonetically different dialects, which change from region to region. You may already begin to see why Norwegian can be a complex second language to master!

Norway is not a member of the European Union (EU) and, despite its current economic stability, was for a period of time one of the poorest countries in Europe. This fact, along with the country's long, dark winters and lack of cultivatable land, means that many traditional Norwegian dishes are humble in ingredients and cooking technique. The focus in traditional Norwegian cuisine is on the quality of ingredients and on preserving techniques, such as curing meats, pickling vegetables and fish, and canning fruits and vegetables.

Norway is governed by a constitutional monarchy, which has been headed by His Majesty King Harald V since 1991. The heir apparent to the Norwegian throne is Crown Prince Haakon Magnus. The current Prime Minister is Erna Solberg.

Norway ranks second to Luxembourg in terms of gross domestic product (GDP) per inhabitant, and most Norwegians enjoy a very high quality of life in economic, political, and social arenas.

Al fresco dining is very popular in Norway during the summer.

Introduction
to Norwegian Cuisine & Norwegian Food Culture

I've written this section to help you learn more about Norwegian cuisine: what Norwegians eat (in general terms), what Norwegians buy in supermarkets, and how to "think" like a Norwegian the next time you sit down to enjoy a meal. This section is meant to be a guide to Norwegian gastronomy and my tips for eating well at the Norwegian table, based on my own research and questions I frequently get on the blog.

What do people in Norway eat?
How can one categorize Norwegian cuisine?

Traditionally speaking, in most regions of Norway, people tended to eat what grew or was raised in their part of the country or what they could grow or raise on their own. Norway is a very long, mountainous country, and transporting foods from coast to coast was a tall order until more recent times. Most of what Norwegians tend to eat therefore depends on where they live and what their lifestyle happens to be.

Norwegian cuisine can be categorized as "rustic" with a strong focus on good-quality raw ingredients. New Nordic cuisine is a more modern spin on traditional ingredients found throughout Scandinavia, and Norwegian chefs are right up there with the best making their mark throughout the region. More traditional Norwegian cuisine focuses on raw ingredients preserved, prepared, and served via time-tested methods like curing, boiling, and canning and enlivened with such traditional flavors as dill, cardamom, and juniper berry.

Breakfast

Weekday breakfasts tend to be hurried and quick, with heavy emphasis on dairy and grains. Weekend breakfasts tend to center around bread or rolls with *pålegg* (the stuff you put on top of bread: sliced cold cuts, cheese, various types of fish) or jam. Smoked salmon is paired with fluffy scrambled eggs. Peanut butter is rare, but becoming more popular. Muesli and cereal are also eaten and served with buttermilk, milk, or yogurt. Milk, various juices, coffee—very strong and dark—are common as well. Bacon and eggs are more common on Sundays or for special occasions.

Lunch

The culturally iconic Norwegian *matpakke* (two open-faced sandwiches—or by U.S. standards, one sandwich, split in half) is still quite the norm for children and adults alike in modern-day Norway. Some adults enjoy a warm canteen lunch during work hours if provided by their

company. In much of the country, eating lunch out in a restaurant is relatively uncommon during work hours but more popular on weekends when meeting friends.

Dinner

This is the biggest meal of the day and usually consists of boiled potatoes, another vegetable, and meat, game, or fish. Chicken dishes are not as common but are gaining in popularity. Dinner is nearly always served with *saus*—a brown or white gravy—especially if potatoes are on the menu. Dark or light *lapskaus,* a Norwegian potato stew, or *brennsnut,* a stew made from leftover meats, rutabaga, carrot, potato and broth, are real treats—especially in winter. *Fiskegrateng* (a baked fish dish), poached salmon, meatballs with brown gravy, *komle* (potato dumplings, also called *klubb, kumle, kompe,* and *rasball*), baked trout, leg of lamb, cold smoked mackerel, and pan-fried cod are all common dinner entrees.

Much like the American tradition, Sunday dinner with extended family hasn't completely disappeared but has become less common as people have moved further away from each other. Sundays almost always include a trip to Mom and Dad's (or Grandma's) for cake and coffee.

Frozen convenience foods are very popular in Norway and Norwegians buy more frozen pizza than any other country in Europe.

Fårikål and the Search for a New National Dish

Fårikål, a dish made from boiled lamb, cabbage, and whole peppercorns, has been the national dish of Norway since 1972. Today, Food and Agriculture Minister Sylvi Listhaug wants Norwegians to think deeply about their national dish, as well as their regional specialties. In celebration of the bicentenary of the signing of the Norwegian constitution, Listhaug launched a contest in January 2014 to find out what Norwegians consider their new national dish and to learn which dish each region of Norway celebrates most. Contest entries must be sourced from ingredients produced in Norway.

The contest, which has its own Facebook page called "*Norges nasjonalrett* 2014," started no less than a firestorm, with some asking for Listhaug's resignation instead. Others wondered whether the new national dish would reflect the more recent immigrant groups in Norway. In the end, the contest results proved *fårikål* was still the nation's most beloved dish, receiving 45% of the ballots cast and beating out dishes such as Norwegian meatballs in brown sauce, *lapskaus, fiskeboller* (fish balls) in white sauce, and poached salmon.

Desserts and Cakes

The sweet dishes served after dinner normally fall into two categories in Norway: desserts and cakes. Cakes are not exclusive to after dinner, but desserts generally are. At fancy events

like weddings and major birthday parties, both desserts and cakes are typically served. Desserts are usually heavy in dairy—so be aware if you are lactose intolerant. Ice cream is always a winner and a summer staple, with vanilla the most popular flavor. Some great cakes to try are *bløtkake* (layers of sponge cake, raspberry jam, and whipped cream), *suksesskake* ("success cake"), or *verdensbeste* ("the best cake in the world").

In-Between Meals

Warm waffles served with brown cheese or sour cream and jam are a nice treat and are common at family functions, during the skiing season, or just about any other time of year. Some eat waffles with sausages and hot dogs, a tradition in the southeastern part of the country but popping up in other parts of Norway, as well. *Boller,* Norway's version of sweet buns, are cardamom-scented chunks of gluten-filled heaven. They are sold in raisin, chocolate, and plain varieties. Slices of bread with various spreads on top are also popular as in-between meals, as well.

Coffee

Norwegians drink more coffee than anyone else in the world. They like their coffee very strong by American standards and nearly always black. If you like milk and sugar with your coffee, be sure to ask for it. Tea is normally served alongside coffee on most occasions, but not always. Common types are Earl Gray and Darjeeling.

Regional Differences and Specially Protected Foodstuffs

I live in Stavanger, on the southwestern coast of Norway, which means I and other locals eat a lot of seafood, along with lamb and locally grown produce. Stavanger is located just outside of Jæren, the "food basket" of Norway. Jæren is one of the regional districts in Norway responsible for producing a considerable amount of the country's produce and livestock. Most supermarkets carry produce grown within the local area, and Norwegians are quite good about embracing locally produced goods. Besides Jæren, other regions with a sizable food footprint are Valdres, located in the southern part of central Norway, and Røros, located two hours by train from Trondheim and close to the Swedish border.

Norway has developed the *Beskyttet geografisk betegnelse,* a set of agricultural guidelines that protect the economic interests of producers of various foodstuffs. These guidelines make it illegal for foods that do not follow the guidelines to be labeled as such products. For example, organic *tjukkmjølk* (a thick, sour milk product) from Røros Dairy is the only dairy product that can be called *tjukkmjølk* anywhere in the world. Lamb from Kvitsøy, *fenalår* (cured leg of lamb), potatoes from Ringeriks, and *festsodd* (a stew made from root vegetables and meat) from Trøndelag are all examples of specially protected foodstuffs.

Beer, Spirits, and Other Things Adults Drink

Norwegians (and most Europeans) like to enjoy themselves, when socially appropriate, with a good swig of brew. For many here, drinking is done on the weekends only and, by American standards, may be viewed as excessive. That said, because people tend to drink only on Fridays and Saturdays, the total volume drunk in a week(end) is comparable to hitting happy hour two or three nights a week. This varies, of course, by age, lifestyle, and region.

People of drinking age tend to consume first at house gatherings known as *førspiels* (pre-parties) and then hit the town to keep the vibe going. Beer is common (usually pilsner-style beer), as is wine. Spirits are more often consumed at home or during a night on the town for a special event as they are more expensive at bars and pubs. Cognac is commonly drunk during the colder months and aquavit reigns supreme around Christmas, especially with traditional Norwegian Christmas food. All wine, spirits, and beer containing more than 4.5% alcohol is sold at state-run stores called the *vinmonopolet* or *'pole.*

Snacks and Sweets

Norwegians love chocolate. A lot. They tend to eat most of it during the weekends and during outdoor activities. The iconic Kvikk Lunsj candy bar (similar to the American Kit Kat bar) and pick-and-mix candy sold in bulk are sugary high points for kids and adults. Marzipan is common at Christmas and Easter.

Key Ingredients in Norwegian Cuisine

There is a lot of talk about traditional and new Norwegian cooking these days but historically, Norwegian food has been characterized by a modest list of raw ingredients preserved in various ways. Today, most Norwegian foods and even dishes are the result of preservation methods that render refrigeration unnecessary, such as salt curing, pickling, and canning. Although nowadays refrigerators are commonplace, the legacy of such methods of food preservation is easily recognized.

Fish

In more modern times, some have focused on salmon as a staple item but cod—usually dried and salted—is what put Norway on the map. Locally, at one point, cod was so common and plentiful that workers were paid a cod ration as a part of their weekly salary. Dried, salted cod, also called *klippfisk,* is used in *bacalao* (a fish stew) or in *klippfisk* balls.

Cod, fresh and salted, helped pave the way for many coastal towns in Norway economically speaking and even today is regarded as some of the best in the world. Seafood is one of the country's largest industries, with 2.5 to 3 tons farmed and caught in Norwegian waters every year.

In additional to cod, salmon (fresh, smoked, or served as gravlax), trout, and other seafoods such as mussels, crab, shrimp, prawns, sardines, and mackerel are very common, especially in spring and summer. Pickled herring is very popular, particularly during Christmas.

Dairy Products

Norwegians seriously dig dairy products. And by dig, I mean they serve dairy products—and lots of them—at every meal of the day and as simple, no-fuss desserts year-round. In Norway, milk with varying amounts of fat in it (milk reserved especially for coffee, plus whole, light, super light, and something I find to be more akin to water—sorry, but that's true!), heavy cream (*fløte*), yogurt, butter, and of course *brunost* are sold nearly everywhere one can purchase groceries. *Brunost,* caramelized whey that is better known as brown cheese, is sold in every grocery store and supermarket. It's also starting to gain a following outside of Norway, as international chefs are falling in love with the stuff.

Flours & Grains

Norwegians like variety when it comes to grain products, as evidenced by the wide range of grain types sold as flour in most supermarkets. Ones to try include spelt, rye, barley, "all-purpose" bleached wheat flour, whole-wheat flour, and high-gluten bread flour, among others.

Flatbreads have existed in Norway for eons and are usually pan fried. Unleavened *lefse* come in thin, thick, and potato varieties, each with its own special use or commonly accompanying dish.

Whether in loaves or rolls, fresh or frozen, yeasted bread is an integral part of the modern Norwegian diet and you will find it everywhere. Norwegians rate their yeasted bread on a scale which indicates the percentage of grain kernel in the flour used, which ranges from fine to extra rough. More fermented breads like sourdough are newer additions to the buffet of offerings in most places, but have been gaining popularity. Danish-style rye bread is common in Norway and a good option if you are watching calories or carbohydrates. Gluten-free options are quite good and common in most cities. Ask for these if you have a gluten sensitivity.

Fresh and Cured Meats, Plus a Few Words About Poultry

Norwegians love their meats, both fresh and cured (salt cured and air dried). Sometimes they like their meats a little on the "was fresh, then cured, and is now fresh again" side: Some dishes are based on meats that have been salt cured, then reconstituted, like the mutton dish *pinnekjøtt*. In Norway, you can easily find chicken, pork, and beef in most stores.

Norwegian lamb is considered some of the best in the world due to its taste, texture, and the farming methods used in production. Rogaland County is especially known for its lamb, and many estimate that there may be close to as many lambs living in the area as people. There are several farms raising lamb all over Rogaland County, but special attention is due to the lambs grown on Rennesøy and Kvitsøy due to these regions' history and the unique taste of lamb raised near the sea.

Rennesøy is home to Klostergård, a farm dating back more than 1,000 years, which raises sheep, lambs, and pigs. The farm sits next to Utstein Kloster, the only fully preserved medieval monastery in Norway. Today, the farm is run by husband-and-wife duo Anders Schanche Rettedal and Inger Lise Aarrestad Rettedal.

Kvitsøy lamb (*Kvitsøylam*) is unique and very special due to its distinct taste. It is slightly salty, an effect of the sheep and lambs feeding on grass growing so close to the sea. The taste of *Kvitsøylam* is so unique that it is, in fact, a protected class of meat in Norway and worldwide due to the *Beskyttet geografisk betegnelse* regulations. These branding and production guidelines ensure that the consumer knows that the product she or he is buying is of the highest quality and has been produced under stringent standards. Thus, only producers that follow a strict set of guidelines are allowed to label their meat as "*Kvitsøylam*" within Norway and anywhere in the world. To date, the Oslo-based *Beskyttede betegnelser* agency has also protected other lamb products such as Norwegian *fenalår* and *Lofotlam* (lamb from Lofoten).

Whole fresh or frozen turkeys (for American Thanksgiving and Christmas celebrations) as well as duck are easily found in cities such as Stavanger and Oslo but may be hard to come by in smaller towns. Off cuts of meat (tails, ears, feet, livers, hearts, and other organs) are found at nicer butchers or upscale supermarkets.

Vegetables and Fruits

One thing you can always count on eating in Norway, no matter where you live, is boiled potatoes. Potatoes in Norway are usually boiled in slightly salted water and skinned before serving. I'm not a food anthropologist, but I've been told that boiled potatoes have always been popular because they are relatively easy to prepare, inexpensive, filling, and easily grown in the soil conditions found in many parts of Norway. People often joke that potatoes are served at every meal—even with pasta. Truth be told, they oftentimes are.

Cabbage, rutabaga, and carrots are grown in Norway and are quite common at various meals throughout the day. Norway specializes in root vegetables, so expect those to be in top-quality condition in most markets, while some imports will leave something to be desired. Brussels sprouts are grown in Norway as well as imported.

Norwegian strawberries are the best in the world. No, not kidding. Also worth trying are wild Norwegian blueberries (picked yourself, of course!), blackberries, *multe* berries (also called cloud berries), *lingon* berries (a variety of cranberry), and red current berries. Norwegian apples come in many varieties but the ones from the Hardanger region have a unique flavor and are protected by law. Hardanger produces in excess of 40% of the nation's fruit, with plums, pears, cherries, red currants, and apples most abundant.

Herbs and Seasonings

Dill, parsley, salt, black pepper, juniper berries, cardamom, dried ginger, and paprika are common flavors. Norwegians tend to like their food on the (very) mild side, so don't expect anything labeled as "spicy" to actually be spicy. Spicy in this context usually means your tongue might tingle a bit (I said *might*), but you'll never, ever have to call the fire department.

Jam and Other Spreads

I've included jam and *pålegg* (toppings for bread, such as sliced cold cuts, cheese, and fish) in their own section to highlight the importance of their place in Norwegian cuisine. In former times, jam was an integral part of the Norwegian diet as it was one of the main ways of consuming antioxidant- and vitamin-C-rich berry fruits in winter.

Holidays and Celebrations

New Year

After a month of hustle and bustle with Christmas, New Year celebrations are a welcome time of relaxation and reflection. Traditions vary from region to region, but Norwegians mostly meet with friends for partying on New Year's Eve and then with immediate family for a nice supper on New Year's Day. Supper items vary, but influences from across Europe and the States are quite common. Turkey is increasingly eaten on New Year's Day, as is *pinnekjøtt*, cod, *lutefisk* (gelatinous cod), and other yummies one might expect at Christmas.

Easter: A Break from the Darkness and A Time to Go Skiing

The Norwegian Easter lamb tradition goes back centuries and has its roots in the religious and biblical traditions of Easter, the holiday that commemorates the resurrection of Jesus after his crucifixion by the Romans.

Easter dinner in Norway means serving *rakfisk* (salted, fermented fish) and lamb, or more recently *skinke* (ham) or *pinnekjøtt*. Particularly popular cuts of lamb during this holiday are leg of lamb (*lammestek*), lamb shanks, lamb chops, and a variety of lamb stews.

The most common form of lamb prepared for Easter dinner is leg of lamb. Most stores begin to stock leg of lamb in the beginning of the month in which Easter falls. Most of the legs sold in stores during Easter time are from frozen lambs from the previous year's slaughter or from lambs born late in the previous calendar year and slaughtered in January/February of the current year, then frozen and sold a few months later at Easter time.

Lamb isn't in season in Norway during Easter due to the preceding lengthy and dark winter in Norway, and its impact on the mating season and birthing season. Breeding season usually runs from October to December. Sheep and lamb are grazing animals, which means they need grass to feed on, and due to the long, dark winter, the grass on which they feed on hasn't quite grown back yet in time for lambs to be of slaughtering size by Easter. The weather and climate also impact why Norwegian lamb is in season during autumn, not spring, as it is in many other parts of the world. This is also why the sheep and lambs raised in Rogaland tend to gestate, be born, and grow to slaughtering size sooner than their northern counterparts. Norwegians eat on average 6 kilos (just over 13 pounds) of lamb per person in a year.

Here are a few more facts about Easter in Norway:

1. A very traditional Easter supper eaten throughout most of Norway is *rakfisk,* not lamb or ham. *Rakfisk* is a fermented fish dish made from fresh trout. It is traditionally served sliced on *flatbrød* or *lefse* and topped with raw onion and sour cream.

2. Norwegians eat 20 million oranges during Easter every year. Some believe this tradition began as a result of merchant ships returning to Norway during Easter time with the year's first harvest from southern Europe. Also, as oranges are high in vitamin C, they are quite appreciated after the long and dark winter.

3. Eggs are a symbol of rebirth and chickens are a symbol of fertility, which is why both are symbols of Easter in Norway (and elsewhere). Eggs prepared in a variety of ways and egg-based dishes are common during Easter.

4. The most popular chocolate eaten during this time of year is the iconic Kvikk Lunsj. Kvikk Lunsj was created in 1937 and has been in production every year since, excluding 1941–1949 due to the Second World War. It's reported that Norwegians eat on average nine Kvikk Lunsj a year, three during the Easter period.

Syttende Mai (May 17)—Norwegian Constitution Day

Syttende Mai is an annual celebration of all things Norwegian. The year 2014 marked the 200th anniversary of Syttende Mai, or the 17th of May as it colloquially called. Syttende Mai celebrations all over the world were extra special this year, as the nation celebrated the day the Norwegian constitution was signed in Eidsvoll, Norway, in 1814.

Although condemned in its early years by first the Swedish and then the Norwegian king, this celebration of Norwegian statehood marks one of the occasions every year when Norwegians wear their traditional outfits called *bunads,* take to the streets in parades, and celebrate with family (plus eat lots of cakes and drink strong, dark coffee).

History. Syttende Mai, or Constitution Day (Grunnlovsdagen) as it is more formally called, marks the day the Norwegian constitution was signed and celebrates Norway's declaration as an independent nation from Sweden, although full independence would come in 1905.

Parades. Every city and town in Norway has at least a children's parade to celebrate Syttende Mai. Children march down the streets of their neighborhood in *bunads* or their best formal clothing, waving flags or playing their instruments if they are part of their school's marching band. In larger cities, such as Stavanger, there is also commonly a parade for the adults in town to march in celebration of Syttende Mai. The largest parade on is in Oslo, the Norwegian capital, and includes more than 75 schools and marching bands. The Oslo parade route includes a trip past the Royal Palace, where the Norwegian royal family greets parade participants and passers-by from the main balcony.

Outside of Norway, Norwegians and Norwegian descendants all over the world celebrate Syttende Mai. The largest population of Norwegian emigrants traveled to the U.S., which

means the U.S. also has the largest Syttende Mai parades outside of Norway. In the U.S., parades, speeches, and fun runs are held in towns and cities with sizable Norwegian emigrant populations such as Seattle, Washington; Brooklyn, New York; Stoughton, Wisconsin; Minneapolis, Minnesota; and Billings, Montana. The Syttende Mai parade in Seattle lays claim to being the third-largest in the world behind Bergen and Oslo.

Ice cream, hot dogs, and lots of cakes. Norwegians celebrate Syttende Mai by eating ice cream (*is* in Norwegian) and hot dogs (*pølse*) during the parades or shortly after. Later in the day, after the parades have finished, Norwegians tend to gather with other family members for *smørbrød* (open-faced sandwiches) served with milk, juice, and carbonated water, as well as coffee and tea. Several varieties of cakes are also served on Syttende Mai, including the classic *bløtkake* (a cousin to the very British Victoria sponge), *suksesskake* ("success cake") and *verdensbeste* ("the best cake in the world"). More coffee is served, of course, to help wash it all down.

The end of russ-ing. *Russ* is a special Norwegian phenomenon, which can only be described as tolerated social mischief. "*Russ*" are students in their last year of high school who wear self-decorated red or blue overalls and spend about a month acting mischievous all over town. Many *russ* spend their month of debauchery drinking heavily and causing trouble. The phenomenon started as way for students to blow off steam after years of studying but has evolved into the Norwegian version of April Fools' Day–meets–Spring Break.

During the month of *russ,* usually beginning about six weeks before Syttende Mai, students play tricks on their classmates and neighbors, drive around in old vans playing very loud music, steal street signs, and commit other acts of social defiance. They also pass out cards with their photo and information on them, to trade like baseball cards. *Russ* are tolerated for the most part by the police and local community until May 17, when all *russ* activities are supposed to end and students return to their normal, calm selves.

Confirmation

Confirmation in Norway has historically been a time when Norwegians are confirmed as full-fledged members of the Church of Norway. The act of being confirmed also has social implications, as being confirmed is seen as a rite of passage for Norwegians when they turn 15. After a series of confirmation classes on values and ethics, a confirmation ceremony takes place inside a church, or in a civil ceremony for non-religious Norwegians. The ceremony is held for large groups of Norwegians at once. The practice of holding non-religious civil confirmation ceremonies has been growing in popularity since the first civil confirmation ceremony was held in Oslo in 1951.

A home or hotel reception usually follows the confirmation ceremony and includes immediate and extended family, as well as friends of the family and even neighbors. During the reception, alcohol is normally not served, but one can look forward to a buffet dinner or a tapas-like meal, or even open-faced sandwiches. The reception includes several varieties of cakes, strong coffee, and rounds of speeches from parents and grandparents.

Confirmation gifts are a hot topic of discussion these days in the Norwegian media. Cash gifts (some youngsters walk away from confirmation with upwards of US$5,000), *bunads* for girls

(costing on average US$8,000–$10,000) and expensive vacations abroad have been come increasingly usual as the average citizen's wealth has increased. Some have questioned all of this extravagance, while others have embraced it.

Christmas—the Most Wonderful Time of the Year

The Christmas season is a unique time of year in Norway, filled with many heartfelt and highly anticipated activities. Norway's best dishes are served during the Christmas season, commonly with aquavit. *Pinnekjøtt*, *medisterkaker* (Christmas meatballs), *ribbe* (pork belly), cod, stewed red cabbage, *julepølse* (Christmas sausage), *lutefisk*, reindeer steak, dried and cured meats, pickled fish, boiled potatoes, boiled carrots, and other dishes are common during Christmas dinner (served on the evening of December 24.)

Norwegians believe serving less than seven types of cookies at once is bad luck, so it is usual to find several varieties to choose from when visiting family and friends. Cakes and cookies are made with real butter, and *multe* (cloud berry) cream desserts are highly prized.

For some, the most highly anticipated event of the work-life social calendar is the annual company Christmas party, better known as the company *julebord*. This is the event where company employees share Christmas cheer (*julefryd*) and salute a productive year together. The event oftentimes includes pre-drinks, dinner and dessert, and some form of entertainment. Speeches by employees are also quite usual.

The literal English translation of the word *julebord* is "Christmas table." *Julebord* festivities grew out of the Norwegian tradition of an annual company Christmas feast served at a long, rectangular table.

This yearly event is the one time all of the company's employees are sure to "let their hair down," relax, and have a good time building social bonds with each other. The event is often held at a hotel or restaurant and can range from casual to quite formal. The norm, however, is somewhere in between, or more semi-formal. The night is broken into various stages, including welcome drink/pre-drink, dinner, speeches by company employees, dessert and coffee, then entertainment.

A before-dinner beverage, a pre-drink or a welcome drink, is usually served at the bar of the location holding the event or in the lobby or sitting room of the restaurant. Here guests are usually served champagne or a typical Norwegian Christmas drink, a mulled wine called *gløgg*. *Gløgg* is warm spiced wine served in a coffee mug, with slivered almonds and raisins at the bottom. A small snack such as *pepperkake* (gingerbread cookies) may also be served alongside the warm *gløgg*. This is the time to drink, be merry, and have casual conversation to "warm up" for the night. When the dinner portion of the event begins, diners are asked to take their seats and are given a formal welcome by one of the company/department bosses or managers. The chef who prepared the dinner menu may also introduce the food, explaining what's on offer and how the meal will be served.

Some *julebord* events include a men's speech and/or a women's speech, normally a humorous account of life from the male or female point of view. There may also be speeches given to highlight a special event at the company, recognize group achievements and milestones, and generally prep the guests for the fun night ahead. The tone of the night is light-hearted and fun, so the speeches and any presentations given will be light in tone, as well.

Food Shopping In Norway

Over on the *Thanks for the Food* blog, I get a lot of questions from expatriates (expats for short) about the differences in shopping for groceries here in Norway versus their home country. Food shopping in Norway has changed considerably in the last ten years. In former times, product variety was low and customer service was poor at best by American standards. A lot has changed (and continues to change) here though, notably the places in which the general public buys groceries.

Where to Shop

Full-service supermarkets. Theses stores have separate seafood, meat, and bakery sections (and staff trained in each area). They tend to sell a large selection of imported and national beer brands, have an extensive baking section, and sell higher-end products. They tend to be large and resemble similar-sized stores in the U.K. and U.S.

Few-frills grocery stores. These stores are smaller and are more common in Norway because there are fewer serviced areas. They are usually staffed with persons who do not have specialized training in seafood, meats, or bakery items and pastries. The selection of food items sold in these stores is usually quite small in comparison to full-service supermarkets.

International food stores. Turkish, Asian, and other "foreign" shops tend to be better places than Norwegian stores to buy fruits, vegetables, spices, beans, grains like rice and bulgur, and oils. They also tend to carry foods from more than one region of the world, and some also sell fresh meats, like lamb. Prices in these types of stores vary, as does quality. If you find an international store you like, try asking for their delivery days to ensure you get the freshest items they carry as soon as possible.

Mathallen, farmers markets, and farms. Depending on where you are in Norway, the market tradition is either coming back in full force or never fully faded out. Mathallen Oslo is a great place to stop in for specialty Norwegian and imported items. Other *mathallen* (market or food hall) projects are popping up in Norway, as well, so keep your eyes open for those. Farmers markets in most major cities are operated by Bondes Marked or are local initiatives such as Stavanger's Marked i Sentrum project. Farms are also great places to shop for eggs, fresh produce, meats, and other goods. Some farms do home delivery for a fee.

Customer Service

The most common questions I've received from readers are related to customer service and product availability. Both are highly impacted by the difficulties in distribution in Norway, import duties and taxes on various classes of imported foods, and overall product demand. (Also, be aware that there are different tax brackets for different items in the grocery stores:

Imported food items are in one bracket, non-imported foods are in another bracket, and non-food items are in yet another.)

1. Open hours in most food stores vary, but nearly all are reduced during the weekend and are shown in brackets on grocery store signs. Stores also have restricted hours during Easter (beginning on the Tuesday before Easter Sunday), as well as during Christmas and New Year.

2. Most grocery stores and food boutiques are closed on Sundays. Some larger cities have special stores that are also open on Sundays; they are restricted in size and therefore have special privileges. Some international stores also have Sunday hours, but not all, so check the stores in your area for open hours.

3. Cashiers tend to swipe your items down the conveyor belt pretty fast here, without making much eye contact in the process. Don't worry: They aren't trying to be rude, they are trying to be efficient and get through your purchases (and the line of shoppers behind you) as fast as possible.

4. No one—and I mean no one—bags your groceries for you in Norway. You must bag your groceries yourself, and walk them out to your car (or bike) on your own, no matter how old you are. Also, you must pay for carrier bags in Norway. Plastic bags at the register must be bought for a small fee (normally 1 Norwegian *krone*) and are usually quite thick compared with the flimsy ones in the U.S. Norwegians tend to bring their own bags to the store, use collapsible crates, or carry items out without a bag. I know, shocking! But Norwegians are pretty environmentally friendly and budget conscious, so reducing the number of plastic bags they use is key.

Product Availability

I tend to get a lot of "where can I find" questions as well, so here are my top tips about product availability in Norwegian supermarkets and other food stores.

1. Stores tend to get routine deliveries every week for certain items, but not for every item. Because of this, when an item runs out—especially a specialty or imported item—it may stay out of stock for longer than you'd expect back home. Be patient, and try to buy a few extras the next time the store has your item in stock. Also, most food stores in Norway don't have sizable stock rooms, which means most of their inventory is "out on the floor" already. Asking an employee to "look in the back" for additional inventory is very uncommon.

2. If you are new to Norway and don't know the Norwegian name of an item, ask for it in English. Bear in mind, however, that some products go by their British English, rather than American English, name.

3. Cilantro is called coriander in Norway. Although technically two different plants, in Norway and throughout most of Europe, coriander is used instead of cilantro in most recipes.

4. Norwegians tend to like their food mild, which means anything sold as "spicy" isn't really spicy. Just be forewarned. "Spicy ketchup" isn't spicy, and neither are any of the other "spicy" products sold here (unless, that is, you go to an "ethnic" store—that's were the real spice is!).

5. Most of what we know as "Italian" food in the U.S. is actually Italian-American food. Italian food in Norway is (obviously) more continental when you get something authentic.

6. Breadcrumbs (*kavring* in Norwegian) are sold as small, uncrushed, toasted rolls instead of in crumb form as is usual in the U.S. Here, you buy toasted rolls whole and crush them on your own. "Seasoned" breadcrumbs not exist in Norway and panko (Japanese breadcrumbs, nowadays pretty common in most U.K. and U.S. supermarkets) are only sold in Asian grocery stores.

7. Fresh tuna in Norway is actually not fresh. It is frozen, then thawed, and is pretty hard to come by in most cities. Your local fish market, full-service supermarket, or nicer fishmonger locations usually have tuna for sale, albeit seasonally.

8. The cuts of meat, especially beef and pork, are not the same in Norway as in the U.S., Germany, or the U.K. Most meats here are cut according to French tradition, some according to Danish and German standards, and some by U.K. or U.S. tradition.

9. Socks, underwear, wool underclothes, and stockings are commonly sold in most places that sell groceries in Norway!

10. Gas stations do not sell alcohol at all, and grocery stores sell limited assortments of lower-alcohol beer. All beer with over 4.5% alcohol content and all other alcohol must be bought in state-run stores called the *vinmonopolet*.

What to Eat During A Visit to Norway

The last few years have opened me up to the beauty of Norwegian gastronomy. Obviously, trying everything you can while visiting Norway isn't always an option, but here is my short list of what to eat if you want to enjoy the good, the better, and the amazing from the Norwegian table.

Norwegian strawberries: Strawberry season is short, but it's a high point in summer. I've never been a huge fan of strawberries but the Norwegian variety is to die for! Try them and see what I mean: Sweet and small, they are a variety you will fall in love with.

Smoked salmon: The best in the world, hands down.

Whale: Very controversial meat and obviously not something for vegans or vegetarians, but a traditional Norwegian food and worth a go if you are so inclined. This is not a menu staple for most restaurants throughout the country, so look for it at food festivals and off the beaten track.

Smalahove: This sheep's head dish looks scary (I suppose food that looks back at you while you eat it has a tendency to do that, right?), but it will definitely make for a good photo opportunity. I hear the cheek cavity contains the best meat.

Lutefisk: Beloved and feared, lutefisk is a Christmas dish many in Norway enjoy. Try it and judge for yourself.

Meatballs: Norwegian "meatcakes" are cousins to the Swedish variety, but better.

Lefse: Norwegian flatbreads, similar to tortillas. Usually served with butter and sugar, sometimes with cinnamon, too. Occasionally made with potato.

Hot dogs and sausages: Norwegians love hot dogs. Stavanger's A. Idsøe butchery is the oldest butcher in Norway and sells the best hot dogs and sausages I've ever had. They are 90%–95% meat plus are gluten free. If you ever make it to Stavanger, pop in for hot dogs (called *pølse* in Norwegian), dried and cured meats, plus excellent Norwegian cold cuts.

Pickled fish: Herring and other types of fish are pickled in Norway and eaten year round but especially during the Christmas season.

Leverpostei: Liver pâté is normally served on brown bread, then topped with sliced red onions or sweet pickles.

Fish pudding and fish balls: The fishy versions of meatloaf and meatballs. Béchamel sauce is a common accompaniment.

The iconic Norwegian matpakke

Thanks *for the* Food

Special Notes
for Vegetarians and Those with Food Sensitivities

I was a vegetarian for almost ten years and I know all too well the pain of eating a peanut butter and jelly sandwich at dinner because there is nothing animal-free to eat. Simply put, it sucks. Here are some tips for veggies and vegans moving to or traveling in Norway.

Gluten Sensitivities

Gluten sensitivities have unfortunately become a reality for more and more of the Norwegian population. The upside to this is that gluten-free options have also become more common over the last ten years. Gluten-free bread is available in nearly every grocery store and supermarket, as is an "allergy" section filled with foods that are certified free of gluten. Health food stores are filled with options, as well, and most cities and towns have them. Some shopping for items can also be done online through Norwegian and international retailers.

Milk Allergies

Due to the high prevalence of milk allergies, soy-based dairy products are becoming more common. Soy, oat, and rice milks are available in many larger grocery stores and supermarkets.

Soy and Other Meat Replacements

Soy and vegetable meat replacements (hot dogs, hamburgers, mince, faux chicken, etc.) are available, but be ready to pay for them. They tend to be pricy and can be hard to find outside of the four major cities (Oslo, Bergen, Trondheim, Stavanger). Instead, try some of the online retailers.

If you'll be in the larger cities, look in the freezer and produce sections of major grocers. Health food stores usually stock some items, but selection may be limited.

Tofu

Tofu (silken and firm varieties) is available in most major cities. Check out Asian food stores for freshly made tofu and cheaper prices on the packaged stuff. Some major grocery store chains sell packaged tofu (usually the silken variety) in the Asian food section. Also check organic food stores and health food stores. The ingredients to make homemade tofu are easily bought in Norway.

Tempeh and Wheat Gluten

Tempeh and wheat gluten (faux duck) can also be found in health food, Asian, and organic food stores.

Textured Vegetable Protein

I buy dried TVP (textured vegetable protein, used in stews and faux mince–friendly meals) in a store that stocks International foodstuffs or in the health food store.

Veggies

Most grocery stores have a decent selection of vegetables, but seek out greengrocers/produce grocers for the best and widest selection. Most major cities have at least one. Root vegetables are usually Norwegian grown and very good quality.

Nuts and Seeds

Nuts and seeds are often located in the baking section. Sunflower, sesame (white), pumpkin, and linen (flax) seeds, are the most widely available, as well as raw hazelnuts, raw almonds, salted pistachios, and salted cashews. Brazil and pine nuts are also sold, but are not as common. Prices vary between stores, so do your research if you are cost conscious.

Beans and Legumes

Beans and legumes are available in dried, tinned, conventional, and organic form. "Ethnic" and organic grocers sell the widest variety, but tinned garbanzo and red kidney beans are available in most stores.

When a Guest in Someone's Home

If you are eating at someone's home, feel free to mention that you don't eat meat, but also offer your host suggestions on what you do eat or ask if you can bring something to share with the other guests.

When Eating Out

International restaurants, such as those serving Indian or Chinese cuisine, offer more choice for vegetarians and vegans than do more traditional Norwegian ones. Bean and tofu dishes are not commonplace outside of international restaurants, and in some places you will have to ask for a special order sans meat.

Strawberry jam, knekkebrød (page 34), and the perfect boiled egg (page 42)

Breakfast

No-Knead Bread,
aka Lazy Man's Homemade Bread

Also known as "Lazy Man's Homemade Bread," this recipe helped me fall in love with bread again after years of swearing off all "carbs" (bread, potatoes, rice, pasta, etc.). Now I eat bread every day and can't imagine my life without it.

The thing I love about this no-knead bread recipe is its simplicity. In total, minus baking time, the recipe takes five minutes to put together, mostly because the quantities are measured on a scale, not in volume. Measuring quantities in weight versus volume makes baking much more exact and better guarantees a superb end result. I also love this recipe because it includes only four ingredients, all of which can be found in any grocery store.

I bake this bread in a terra cotta clay oven, which gives it a divine crust and soft, sourdough-like interior. The effect of the terra cotta oven is very similar that of a pizza stone: The clay helps the bread bake without burning and helps give it its dynamo crust. Terra cotta ovens can be bought at your local cooking or hardware store. If you don't have (nor want to buy) one, this recipe can be made in a regular metal or glass loaf pan. (If you are using a regular bread pan, preheat the pan for 15 minutes before placing the dough in it, to help ensure a good crust.)

Ingredients

Makes 1 loaf

750 grams (3 cups) flour (white,
    whole wheat, rye, or
    a combination)
1/4 teaspoon active dry yeast
3 teaspoons salt
100 grams (1/2 cup) nuts or
    seeds (such as walnuts, pine
    nuts, pumpkin seeds, flax
    seeds, or sunflower seeds)
600 milliliters (2 1/2 cups) water

Directions

Combine the flour, yeast, salt, and nuts or seeds in a large mixing bowl. Make a well in the center of the flour mixture and pour in the water. Stir until all ingredients are combined and no dry flour remains.

Lightly sprinkle the dough with white flour, then cover the bowl with plastic wrap and allow it to sit in a warm, dry place for 12 to 24 hours. Good places to let the bread rise are near a warm fireplace, near a heating vent, or on a high shelf in the warmest room in your home. The longer the dough ferments, the better the taste. Once the dough has fermented and risen, you are ready to bake.

Place the clay oven inside the oven and preheat at 250° C/480° F for 45 minutes. The clay oven needs to be very, very warm before you place the dough in it.

Once the clay oven is warm, sprinkle plain white flour on the bottom and inside walls to prevent the bread from sticking, and scoop the dough into the clay oven. Cover the clay oven with the lid, and return it to the oven for 50 minutes.

When the baking time is up, carefully remove the clay oven, take off the lid, and remove the bread from the clay oven using a silicone spatula. Dust the extra flour off the bottom of the bread and cool the loaf on a wire rack for at least 30 minutes before serving.

Knekkebrød

Knekkebrød, or crispbread, is a staple food in most Norwegian households and is very quintessentially Norwegian with its no-muss, no-fuss production method, although its roots probably lie in Sweden or Denmark. It is a form of flatbread and resembles anything from sandpaper to a seeded cracker. Historically, *knekkebrød* is known for making the most of the basic ingredients you have on hand. My recipe is made simply with various seeds and grains, flour, water, and salt. That's it. An entire batch of *knekkebrød* can be made in a bit over an hour.

Eaten for breakfast, lunch, or a snack at any time of day, *knekkebrød* can replace regular bread as part of an open-faced sandwich. I tend to put butter and Jarlsberg cheese on mine. I also enjoy my *knekkebrød* topped with a soft goat's milk cheese and raspberry jam. Dress yours up however you like.

This recipe uses proportions rather than specific measurements so the batch can be sized up or down depending upon how much *knekkebrød* you want to produce at once.

Ingredients

1 part whole-wheat flour
2 parts seeds and/or whole
grains (such as sunflower
seeds, pumpkin seeds, flax
seeds, wheat berries, steel-cut
oats, rye berries, or quinoa)
Salt
1 part water

Directions

Preheat your oven to 180° C/350° F.

In a large mixing bowl, combine all ingredients except the water. When the ingredients are well combined, add half the water, stir to incorporate, then add more water little by little. You want the final mixture to be moist but not wet; it should clump easily and resemble wet gravel. If the mixture becomes too wet, you will have to increase the baking time. No biggie— but save yourself the extra wait and mix in the water a little at a time.

Line a baking sheet with parchment paper. Transfer the contents of the bowl to the parchment paper and spread the mixture as thinly as possible. Use a rubber spatula or the back of metal spoon to help flatten the *knekkebrød*. Using a rubber spatula or knife, score the flattened *knekkebrød* to make it easier to break after baking. Place the baking tray in the preheated oven and bake for 1 hour.

Remove the baking sheet from the oven and cool the *knekkebrød* on a wire rack until it is cool enough to handle. Break into pieces, top with your favorite spreads like jam and soft cheese, ham, salami, peanut butter, or just plain butter, and enjoy.

Apple-Pear Refrigerator Jam

Jam is an integral part of many breakfast and lunch routines in Norway. I enjoy jam as much as the next person and find a deep sense of accomplishment in making my own from time to time. Most jam recipes call for lengthy canning processes and commercially produced pectin, but I've developed an easier and simpler recipe for making jam.

This method combines apples, herbs, or other flavor-enhancing goodies with the fruit of your choice and 20 to 30 minutes of patience. No sterilizing jam jars, burning yourself with boiling water, or committing to an entire season's worth of one flavor of jam.

For this recipe, I've combined pears and apples with vanilla and a touch of honey for even more flavor.

Ingredients

Makes 2 medium-sized jars

3 pears, peeled, cored,
    and cubed
3 apples, peeled, cored,
    and cubed
200 grams (1 cup) sugar
1 vanilla bean, split lengthwise
1 teaspoon honey
Zest and juice of one lemon

Directions

Place a small plate in the freezer before you begin making the jam. You will use this at a later stage to test whether the jam has set.

Place half the pears in a medium pot and mash with a potato masher. Add the remaining pears to the pot, along with the rest of the ingredients. On medium-high heat, bring the mixture to a boil, stirring constantly so the pears do not stick to the bottom. Once the pears have started to boil, turn the heat down and simmer for 15 minutes, stirring periodically to keep the pears from sticking.

Remove the plate from the freezer and spoon a small amount of the jam onto it. Run your finger through the jam; if has jelled enough that your finger leaves a clear "path" through the jam, remove the pot from the heat. If the jam is not yet thick and jelled to your liking, rinse the plate and return it to the freezer. Continue to simmer the jam for 3 to 5 minutes longer, then test again. If the jam still has not yet jelled, continue to simmer until it has reached your desired thickness, stirring frequently to prevent sticking, and testing every 3 to 5 minutes.

Once the jam has thickened, spoon it into clean glass jars and allow to cool to room temperature. Once cooled, top the jars with lids. Refrigerate for at least 2 hours before serving. Keep your jam refrigerated and enjoy it within 3 weeks for best flavor and freshness

Strawberry Refrigerator Jam

This jam is a staple in my kitchen, especially in summer when Norwegian strawberries are ripe and are sold rather inexpensively in most grocery stores around Stavanger. Norwegian strawberries are the best I've ever tasted, and this recipe allows their flavor to shine, as the amount of sugar is just enough to help the fruit jell. The lemon juice adds a bit of acidity and complexity to the jam, helping to balance the sugar.

Ingredients

Makes 3 medium-sized jars

500 grams (~1 pound) ripe
    strawberries
200 grams (1 cup) sugar
2 teaspoons freshly squeezed
    lemon juice

Directions

Wash, hull, and quarter the strawberries and place them in a large pot. Top the strawberries with the sugar and lemon juice. Cook over medium heat until tiny bubbles begin to form. Once bubbles begin to form and the strawberries have softened, mash them with a potato masher or the back of a large spoon. Bring to a rolling boil and cook for another 5 to 10 minutes.

Allow the jam to cool slightly, then spoon into clean jars. Screw on the jar lids and refrigerate. Alternatively, allow the mixture to cool completely, then freeze. Refrigerated jam will keep for 2 to 3 weeks. Frozen jam will keep for up to 4 months.

Blueberry Refrigerator Jam

This jam recipe comes in very handy during the summer, when wild blueberries are in abundance. If you can't find fresh seasonal blueberries, frozen ones make a decent substitute. (Be sure to defrost them first in a colander and drain the extra liquid).

Ingredients

Makes 3 medium-sized jars

500 grams (~1 pound) fresh
   blueberries
200 grams (1 cup) sugar
Zest of 1 lemon
5 tablespoons freshly squeezed
   lemon juice

Directions

Wash and dry the blueberries and place them in a large pot. Top the blueberries with the sugar, lemon zest, and lemon juice. Cook over medium heat until tiny bubbles begin to form. Once bubbles begin to form and the blueberries have softened, mash them with a potato masher or the back of a large spoon. Bring to a rolling boil and cook for another 10 to 15 minutes, or until the jam reaches your preferred consistency.

Allow the jam to cool slightly, then spoon into clean jars. Screw on the jar lids and refrigerate. Alternatively, allow the mixture to cool completely, then freeze. Refrigerated jam will keep for 2 to 3 weeks. Frozen jam will keep for up to 4 months.

Homemade Butter

Butter is integral to Norwegian cooking. Norwegians tend to use butter rather than oil in nearly every traditional dish (and, of course, as a spread on bread).

Butter is made from whipping cream, or *fløte*, as it is called in Norwegian. While some of us may struggle with our inner dietitian in order to enjoy cream, most of us can (and in my opinion should) enjoy butter. Not too much—just enough—but enjoy it all the same. Why? Well, first of all, butter is made from "real," natural ingredients (and I'm all about anything all-natural). Butter is usually made from just cream and a bit of salt, both ingredients that are readily available to the home cook.

Second, butter just tastes so darn good, and a little dab will do you. A small knob of butter goes a long way in cooked lentils, spinach dishes, or for spreading on bread. Third, butter is easily made at home with a stand mixer, allowing you to control the quality of the ingredients. So join me, if you dare, in making fresh butter at home.

Ingredients

Makes approximately 200 grams
(7 ounces)

500 milliliters (2 cups) whipping
cream
Salt (optional)

Directions

Pour the cream into the bowl of a stand mixer and mix at low speed until the cream begins to form soft peaks, then turn off the mixer. Scrape down the sides of the mixing bowl with a rubber spatula, then continue mixing. After 1 or 2 minutes, slightly increase the speed of the mixer and keep mixing. You're about halfway there, but remember: Patience wins the race.

Keep a close watch, as the whipped cream will turn clumpy rather suddenly, and liquid will begin to splash about in the bottom of the bowl. The yellowish clump on the bottom of the whisk is butter!

Using a rubber spatula, remove the butter from the whisk and the bowl. It will have the consistency of modeling clay: soft but firm. Knead the butter in your hands for a few minutes, all the while squeezing out more of the cloudy liquid.

To help your butter last longer in the fridge, "wash" it in a cold-water bath after you've kneaded and squeezed it. Fill a large bowl with ice water, submerge the butter in the water, and knead and squeeze 2 or 3 times.

After your butter is squeezed, kneaded, and washed to your liking, it is ready to eat. Using a fork or your stand mixer, you can mix in salt to taste, fresh or dried herbs, ground vanilla beans, minced garlic, or your favorite spices, or enjoy it plain and unsalted. Freeze any butter you won't eat within a few days.

Perfect Boiled Eggs

Growing up, the only time I saw boiled eggs was when my dad made potato salad. Our food tradition was scrambled eggs for breakfast; boiled eggs were reserved for potato salad in the summer. Here in Norway, however, my palate has opened up to boiled eggs—even soft-boiled eggs from time to time—all year round.

This is my method for ensuring my boiled eggs come out perfect every time, whether soft- or hard-boiled. The secret is to use a pot big enough that your eggs won't be crowded, begin with cold eggs from the refrigerator, and use residual heat to cook the eggs. This gives you a bit more control over the cooking temperature and lowers the risk of overcooking the eggs and getting that nasty green ring around the yolks. It took me ages (and several dozen eggs) to perfect this technique, but it works.

Ingredients

Eggs (preferably cold from
    the refrigerator, but room
    temperature is fine)
Cold water

Directions

Place the eggs in a pot big enough that the eggs are not touching each other. Add enough cold water to cover the eggs by about 2.5 centimeters (1 inch).

Bring the water to a boil. Once the water has begun to boil, turn off the heat immediately. Allow the eggs to sit in the water for 4 to 6 minutes for soft-boiled eggs or 8 to 10 minutes for hard-boiled eggs. After the eggs have sat in the hot water for the desired time, run cold water over them to stop them from cooking further. Pat the eggs dry and serve.

Blueberry Smoothie

Blueberries, *blåbær* in Norwegian, are an antioxidant- and vitamin C–rich fruit that can be found in the wild or purchased fresh or frozen in stores all over Norway. In North America, we tend to use blueberries in pancakes and smoothies, but Norwegians like to pick them in the summer and make them into jams, or simply eat them plain or with a touch of cream.

Blueberries taste tart to slightly sweet depending on the species and their ripeness. I really appreciate frozen blueberries in winter, as their phytochemicals and vitamin C content help keep me in good health. They are also said to help fight inflammation and, over the long term, cancer.

For this recipe, I've included both dates and honey for added sweetness, but feel free to leave out one or both and sweeten to your liking.

Ingredients

Makes 2 large smoothies or 3 medium smoothies

200 grams (8 ounces) fresh
   or frozen blueberries
1 or 2 ripe bananas
2 to 4 Medjool dates
2 tablespoons honey
4 tablespoons plain, full-fat
   yogurt

Directions

Place all ingredients in a blender and blend on high until smooth. Pour into glasses, serve, and enjoy.

Lean, Mean, and Green Smoothie

A few years back I got really into drinking smoothies every morning as a way to make sure I had something in my "tank" before I left for work. I've tried smoothies based on hemp milk and cashew milk, but this one, based on vegetables commonly grown in Norway, is my favorite.

This recipe offers a great opportunity to use as many organic fruits and vegetables as you can, since many of the ingredients are on the so-called "Dirty Dozen" list of foods with the highest pesticide loads.

Ingredients

Makes 2 large smoothies or 3 medium smoothies

1 large bag of spinach
2 cucumbers
Half a fresh pineapple, cubed
3 stalks celery, chopped
2 tablespoons coconut oil
250 milliliters (1 cup) coconut water (plain water is also fine)
1 or 2 Medjool dates (optional)

Directions

Place all the ingredients in a blender and blend on high until smooth. Pour into glasses and serve.

Norwegian-Style Muesli

Muesli is a mixed cereal of uncooked grains, dried fruit, nuts, and seeds. It is said to have been created in the early 19th century by Swiss physician and nutritional scientist Maximilian Oskar Bircher-Benner as a way to get his patients to eat more healthfully.

Many Norwegians enjoy muesli as a part of their morning routine, as it is easy to prepare and makes for a satisfying breakfast during the work week. Try substituting whatever dried fruits, seeds, and nuts you have on hand. Serve your muesli with milk, yogurt, or the Norwegian way: with cultured or pro-biotic cow's milk.

Ingredients

Makes approximately 6 cups

*90 grams (1 cup) rolled
    or flaked oats*
90 grams (1 cup) barley
90 grams (1 cup) rye berries
*65 grams (1/2 cup) raw
    sunflower seeds*
*32 grams (1/2 cup) pumpkin
    seeds*
*72 grams (1/2 cup) sesame
    seeds*
*95 grams (1 cup) almonds,
    coarsely chopped*
*230 grams (1 cup) dried fruit,
    chopped*
1 teaspoon ground cinnamon

Directions

Mix all ingredients together and store in an air-tight glass jar.

Pytt i Panne

This recipe is great when my fridge is bulging with leftovers that I wouldn't forgive myself for throwing away. Each of the Nordic countries has several "use up your leftovers" dishes, and this dish is one certainly one of them. *Pytt i panne* is basically potato hash by American terms, but in Norway, it can be oh so much more than pan-fried root vegetables.

The basic recipe for *pytt i panne* includes cubed potatoes, carrots, and other vegetables plus meat leftovers. It is made magical with gherkins (cucumber pickles), pickled beets, or other pickled vegetables, or with a fried egg on top. Feel free to "dress" your *pytt i panne* any way you see fit, or based on what you have on hand.

This dish can be served at any time of day, but I tend to enjoy it during long, relaxed weekend breakfasts or brunches with friends after a night out. Make sure all your vegetables are cut to about the same size to ensure everything cooks evenly.

Ingredients

Serves 2 as a meal or 4 as a snack

2 tablespoons canola, sunflower,
     or other neutral-flavored oil
1 onion, cubed
4 potatoes, cubed
2 carrots, chopped
225 grams (~1/2 pound)
     rutabaga, cubed
Salt and freshly ground black
     pepper
225 grams (~1/2 pound) cooked
     meat (such as meatballs,
     roasted meat, or sausages;
     optional)

Directions

Heat the oil in a large frying pan over medium-high heat for
2 minutes. Add the onions and sauté until they are translucent
and soft. Add the potatoes, carrots, and rutabaga and continue
to sauté for another 3 to 5 minutes. Decrease the heat to
medium and allow the vegetables to cook for another 20
to 25 minutes, or until they pick apart easily with a fork.

If including meat, add the meat to the pan and stir to distribute
evenly. Turn off the heat and cover the pan to warm the meat
without overcooking the vegetables.

To serve, place some of the *pytt i panne* on a plate, top with
the fried eggs, if using, and serve with any other accompaniments
on the side.

Optional Accompaniments

Fried eggs
Gherkins
Pickled beets
Capers
Other pickled vegetables
Prepared mustard (spicy or sweet—your choice)

Grilled Mackerel (page 52)

Lunch

Portuguese Klippfisk Fritters,
aka Bolinhos de Bacalhau

You might be asking yourself why I've included a Portuguese recipe in a Norwegian cookbook, but these fritters are more Norwegian than you might think. Although wildly popular in Portugal and Brazil, they are made from Norwegian dried, salted cod, also known as *klippfisk* in Norwegian, bacalao in English, and *bacalhau* in Portuguese. This recipe dates back to the days when Norwegian cod fed more people outside Norway than it did within the country's borders.

A version of this dish can be found in most restaurants in Stavanger and is commonly served as a light lunch or as an appetizer at parties. Bacalao can be purchased on Amazon if not readily available in your area. This recipe is great to make when you have boiled potatoes in your fridge and you need to use them up, or when you want a more international way to serve dried, salted cod.

Try using your hands instead of a spoon to combine the ingredients. Using your hands (and a lighter touch) will help retain the texture of the fish and better keep the fritters' shape when they are cooked.

Thanks *for the* Food

Ingredients

Makes 12 large or 24 small fritters

1 kilogram (2 1/4 pounds) bacalao

800 grams (1 3/4 pounds) potatoes, peeled, cooked, and cooled completely

1 small to medium onion, finely chopped

2 garlic cloves, finely chopped

1 egg, lightly beaten

Parsley

Pinch of salt

1/2 teaspoon freshly ground black pepper

canola, sunflower, or other neutral-flavored oil for frying

1 lime, sliced into wedges

Directions

Place the dried cod in a large bowl and cover with cold water. Allow the fish to soak for 12 hours, then change the water. Allow the fish to soak for another 12 hours, then drain. Allow the fish to soak for up to 36 hours, changing the water every 12 hours, until the fish is fully reconstituted. After the last draining, dry the fish thoroughly with paper towels and begin breaking it into small chunks. Place the chunks in a bowl and set aside.

Mash the potatoes in a separate bowl, then add to the fish and combine. You want to use your "fairy fingers" here and a rather light touch so the fritters don't come out too dense. Add the parsley, salt, and pepper and mix until well combined.

Using two tablespoons or your hands, shape the mixture into balls. If making this dish for lunch, shape bigger fritters. If making appetizers, shape smaller fritters. Chill the fritters in the refrigerator for 30 minutes.

After the fritters have chilled, fry them in hot oil until golden brown, or about 4 minutes per side. Drain on a paper towel, then serve with lime wedges.

Grilled Mackerel

Mackerel are plentiful around Stavanger in the late spring and summer. While I tend to buy mine at the local fish market, they are a great fish to catch for yourself in the waters along the coasts that surround Rogaland and in the fjords.

Mackerel is a protein-rich fatty fish filled with heart-healthy unsaturated fats and other nutrients. Although a bit strong on flavor, gram per gram, mackerel has fewer calories and less saturated fat and cholesterol than red meat. Mackerel can usually be purchased inexpensively; it is also a "hearty" fish that holds up well on the grill.

This is my method for grilling whole mackerel on the barbeque using indirect heat. Ask your fishmonger to clean the fish for you, or clean them thoroughly if you catch them yourself. Also, be sure you generously coat the fish in salt, as this will help prevent it from sticking to the grill.

Ingredients

Serves 4

4 whole mackerel
Sea salt, for coating
1 lemon, sliced into wedges

Directions

Preheat your grill. Arrange the coals on the grill so you can cook the fish using indirect heat.

Rinse the mackerel well under cold, running water. Gently blot the fish dry with paper towels and coat generously with salt. Some of the salt will fall onto the coals and burn off, but the rest will season the fish and help keep it from burning or sticking to the grill.

Place the mackerel on the grill and leave the lid open. Using indirect heat and leaving the lid open will give you greater control over the cooking time and help prevent overcooking. Grill the fish for 5 minutes, turn the mackerel over, and grill for another 5 minutes, or until the flesh becomes opaque. Once the flesh is opaque, remove the fish from the grill. It should flake apart easily with light pressure from a fork. Squeeze lemon wedges over the fish and serve.

Smoked Salmon Wraps

This recipe is easy to make and is good as an appetizer for your next party or an easy weekend lunch. These salmon wraps can be made ahead and hold up quite well without getting soggy. I normally use homemade *lefse* for this recipe (see page 110 or 112), but flour tortillas make a good substitute if fresh *lefse* is not available in your area.

Most of the smoked salmon sold in the U.S. comes from Alaska, but some Norwegian varieties are available via online retailers such as Amazon. If you don't like smoked salmon, you can substitute smoked trout—another Norwegian specialty—or use *fenalår* (dry-cured leg of lamb).

Ingredients

Serves 3 for lunch or 6 to 10 as an appetizer

3 lefse (page 110 or 112)
  or flour tortillas
Dill- or herb-flavored cream
  cheese (mayonnaise is a good
  alternative)
Smoked salmon, sliced
Lettuce
Red onion, chopped

Directions

Lay the *lefse* or tortilla flat and spread edge to edge with a generous layer of cream cheese (or mayonnaise). On top of the cream cheese, layer the smoked salmon, lettuce, and red onion, but reserve a bit of space at one edge of the *lefse* or tortilla. This will be used to secure the roll.

Starting from one edge, roll the lefse tightly to form a log. Press the reserved edge onto the log to close. Using a sharp knife, slice crosswise into rounds, and serve.

Baked Fish Fingers

Is it just me, or does it seem like time flies by during the week? My weekends tend to pass by with ease but weekdays in my calendar feel like their cramped, overworked cousins. When I have a busy week, I still like to enjoy a nice home-cooked meal, and making baked fish fingers (or fish sticks as they are called in the U.S.) is also a great way to get a warm lunch or dinner on the table in minutes. Cod or halibut is used in this recipe, each of which tends to cook quickly; this dish can be whipped up from start to finish in less than 35 minutes.

Also, this recipe allows you to control all the ingredients. For example, you can use gluten-free breadcrumbs and a gluten-free flour, if you are gluten intolerant. This recipe is family-friendly but can also serve as a great summer appetizer dish for your next get-together. Serve with fresh lemon wedges on the side, homemade ranch dipping sauce or remoulade, and even ketchup if you fancy. Switch up the seasoning in the flour by adding in a little onion powder and garlic powder or smoked paprika. In the rare case that you find yourself with leftovers, freeze them for an easy meal on another day.

Ingredients

Serves 4 as a meal, 6 as a snack

- 1 kilogram (~2 1/4 pounds) boneless cod or halibut fillets, cut into thick strips
- 120 grams (1 cup) all-purpose flour
- 1 teaspoon salt
- 1/2 teaspoon freshly ground black pepper
- 240 grams (2 cups) Japanese panko or regular unseasoned breadcrumbs
- 3 eggs, beaten
- 2 tablespoons canola or sunflower seed oil, or other neutral-flavored oil
- 1 lemon, sliced into wedges

Directions

Preheat the oven to 230° C/450° F. Line a baking sheet with parchment paper and set aside.

In a large bowl, combine the flour, salt, and pepper; set aside. In another bowl, beat the eggs; set aside. Place the breadcrumbs in a separate bowl and set aside. You should now have three bowls ready for dredging the fish.

First, dip a strip of fish into the egg mixture to coat, then dredge with the flour mixture, then dip back into the egg mixture. Finally, dredge the fish strip in the breadcrumbs and place on the baking sheet. Follow this procedure with each strip until the baking tray is full, but make sure the fish strips are not touching each other.

Brush the oil on top of each fish finger and bake for 10 minutes. Turn each fish finger once, brush with oil, and bake until golden brown, about 5 to 7 more minutes. Serve with fresh lemon wedges on the side and your choice of dipping sauces.

Open-Faced Shrimp Sandwiches
with Homemade Mayonnaise

Norway (like Scandinavia as a whole) is quite fond of the open-faced sandwich. In contrast to the American sandwich tradition, sandwiches in Norway are often prepared as a single slice of bread smeared with butter, then topped with *pålegg* (a general name given to sandwich fixings such as sliced cheeses, cold cuts, and sandwich spreads) and the occasional condiment, such as mayonnaise, and eaten with a knife and fork.

This type of sandwich sounds minimal but can be quite satisfying and is an easy way to serve a large group in a hurry with no fuss. The art of open-faced sandwiches lies in layering your toppings of choice on your bread in such a way that each bite includes a taste of every topping.

My favorite open-faced sandwiches are topped with, in order:

Butter
Lettuce
Cucumber
Fresh peel-and-eat shrimp (boiled in salt water)
Sliced red onion
Homemade mayonnaise
A light dusting of freshly ground black pepper
A squeeze of fresh lemon juice

Try your hand at making open-faced sandwiches with your favorite combinations and fresh homemade *majones* (mayonnaise). This recipe takes just 20 minutes to prepare.

Mayonnaise

Makes 1 cup

250 milliliters (1 cup) canola
    or sunflower seed oil, or other
    neutral-flavored oil
1 egg (include an extra yolk for
    a richer mayo)
2 tablespoons white wine
    vinegar or lemon juice
1 tablespoon water
1/4 teaspoon dry mustard
    powder
1/2 teaspoon sugar
1/2 teaspoon salt

Directions

Using an immersion blender on high speed, combine all ingredients until emulsified. Store mayonnaise in an air-tight container in the refrigerator for up to 2 weeks.

Crab Salad with Dill and Chives

Crab salad is very commonly eaten in summer when the temperature rises and the long summer evenings bring visitors to Norwegian homes until well into the night.

Crab salad is something I've fallen in love with since I moved to Norway, especially because fresh crab meat is pretty amazing here and is available in most grocery stores. This recipe will help your kitchen stay cool this summer and keep you feeling full but not heavy.

Ingredients

Serves 4

300 grams (10 1/2 ounces) cooked white crab meat, shredded (use imitation crab if good-quality crab meat isn't available in your area)

300 milliliters (1 cup) mayonnaise (sour cream is a good substitute)

2 tablespoons fresh chives, finely chopped

2 tablespoons fresh dill, finely chopped

2 tablespoons freshly squeezed lemon juice

Salt and freshly ground white pepper

Directions

Combine the crab meat, mayonnaise, chives, dill, and lemon juice in a large bowl and season to taste with salt and pepper. Be careful to fold, not mix, as you do not want to mash the crab meat together. Allow the salad to chill for at least 30 minutes before serving. Serve over bread or lettuce leaves.

Steamed Mussels

This is definitely one of those easy-to-prepare lunches that will impress any guest (so long as they eat shellfish). The best way to serve these mussels is outdoors on a breezy, sunny afternoon, with a bottle of white wine and loads of crusty bread (so you can enjoy the mussels casually and sop up all the broth). A nice touch: Provide each guest with a small bowl of warm water and a few slices of lemon for cleaning and freshening their hands after lunch.

Ingredients

Serves 4 to 6

3 tablespoons butter

1 shallot, minced

250 milliliters (1 cup) dry white wine

1 1/2 kilograms (~3 pounds) mussels, cleaned

Large handful of fresh parsley, chopped

Freshly ground black pepper

Directions

In a medium pot, melt butter over medium heat. Add the shallots and sauté until translucent. Pour in the wine and add the mussels. Increase the heat to medium-high and cover. Steam the mussels until the shells open, approximately 5 minutes.

Once the shells have opened, remove the mussels from the pot, sprinkle with parsley, and season with pepper to taste. Serve immediately, with crusty white bread on the side.

Komle (page 72)

Dinner

Halibut with Bacon Drippings
with Oven-Baked Finger Potatoes

Halibut is a quite elegant-tasting (albeit ugly) fish and is made hearty and slightly rustic when cooked in bacon drippings, of all things. I like to cook this for my family when they visit from Arizona, or for friends when they travel to Norway from abroad.

I'm a little bit "old school" in that I collect the drippings every time I cook bacon, just like my grandmother did, so I always have some on hand. This recipe makes great use of those drippings, but if you don't have bacon drippings readily available, you can always fry up a packet of bacon before getting started, use the drippings in this recipe, then crumble the bacon over the halibut.

Ingredients

Serves 6

4 (125-gram/4 1/2-ounce)
    halibut fillets
Salt and freshly ground black
    pepper
3 tablespoons bacon drippings

Directions

Season halibut steaks with salt and pepper. Warm the bacon drippings in a frying pan. Add the fish and fry over medium heat until one side is lightly browned, about 5 minutes. Flip the fish and cook for another 3 to 5 minutes, or until lightly browned on the second side. Remove the fillets from the pan and allow to rest for 5 minutes before serving.

Oven-Baked Finger Potatoes

500 grams (~1 pound) fingerling
    potatoes, halved lengthwise
3 tablespoons olive oil
1 teaspoon freshly ground black
    pepper
1 teaspoon salt

Preheat the oven to 200° C/390° F and line a baking sheet with parchment paper. In a medium bowl, drizzle the potatoes with olive oil and add the pepper and salt. Toss the potatoes, making sure to evenly coat them with the olive oil and seasonings. Place the potatoes on the baking sheet and bake for 25 to 30 minutes, or until they are soft when pierced with a fork. Serve with the halibut, and enjoy.

Salmon Fish Cakes
with Apple and Carrot Salad

Norwegian fish cakes are traditionally made with cod or a similar type of white fish, but I like to make mine with salmon instead. Salmon is more flavorful and healthful than cod, especially wild-caught salmon.

Ingredients

Makes 12 small or 6 medium fish cakes

500 grams (~18 ounces) fresh salmon fillet, skinned and deboned

30 grams (1/4 cup) potato flour

2 teaspoons sea salt

200 milliliters (3/4 cup) milk

1 egg

1 teaspoon baking powder

3 tablespoons butter for frying

3 tablespoons canola or sunflower seed oil, or other neutral-flavored oil

Directions

Place all ingredients except butter and oil in a food processor and pulse at medium speed until fairly smooth. Some fish chunks may remain, but the mixture should have a relatively consistent texture. Wet hands with water and shape the dough into patties.

Apple and Carrot Salad

2 apples, grated

4 carrots, grated

Freshly squeezed lemon juice

Freshly ground black pepper

Salt

Combine the grated apple and carrots in a medium bowl. Season to taste with lemon juice, salt, and pepper.

Italian Baked Cod

I absolutely adore cod. This recipe for Italian baked cod is a fab way to cook it if you can get your hands on good-quality cod from your fishmonger. Serve this dish with rice, quinoa, potatoes, or a simple side salad.

Ingredients

Serves 4

2 tablespoons olive oil
325 milliliters (1 1/2 cups) of
    your favorite marinara sauce
4 (125-gram/4 1/2-ounce) cod
    fillets
Parmesan cheese, for topping

Directions

Coat the bottom of a baking dish with olive oil. Cover the bottom of the dish with half the marinara sauce. Lay the cod fillets in the dish, on top of the marinara sauce. Top the fillets with the remaining sauce.

Bake for 20 to 25 minutes, or until the fish is firm when touched with a fork and flakes easily. Remove the dish from the oven and top the fish with Parmesan cheese.

Fiskegrateng

Fiskegrateng is a classic Norwegian baked fish and pasta dish. Think of it as baked macaroni and cheese with cod and green peas mixed in, to boot. This recipe calls for regular macaroni, but if you are watching your carb intake (and who isn't these days?!), try using whole-wheat macaroni instead. A word to the wise: Go easy on the nutmeg if you are grating or grinding your own. A little goes a long way, and you just need a pinch to give your sauce that "Hmmmm . . . what is *that*?" kick.

Consider this a great weekday dinner for a family or something easy to make for a potluck dinner.

Ingredients

Serves 6

250 grams (~2 cups) macaroni

3 tablespoons butter

4 tablespoons all-purpose flour

400 milliliters (1 1/2 cups) milk

100 grams (1 cup) Jarlsberg
    cheese, grated

1/4 teaspoon ground nutmeg

Salt and pepper to taste

400 grams (~1 1/4 pounds)
    deboned cod fillet, uncooked,
    skinned, and cut into small
    cubes

125 grams (~1 cup) green peas

125 grams (1 cup) dry
    breadcrumbs

Directions

Boil the macaroni in a large pot of salted water until al dente, about 7 minutes. Drain, rinse with cold water, and set aside. Be careful to not overcook the pasta, as it will cook again in the oven and you do not want the final result to be mushy.

Preheat the oven to 200° C/390° F.

In a medium pot, slowly melt the butter over medium heat. When the butter is almost fully melted, whisk in the flour to form a paste. Allow the paste to cook for 1 or 2 minutes, then add the milk and whisk until smooth. Cook for 2 to 3 minutes, or until the sauce begins to thicken slightly.

Next, add a small handful of the cheese to the pot and stir. Allow the cheese to melt a bit, stir, then add another small handful of cheese. Repeat until all the cheese is melted and well incorporated into a smooth sauce. Stir in the nutmeg and season with salt and pepper to taste. Set aside and allow to cool for 5 minutes.

To assemble the dish, pour the macaroni into a baking dish and layer the peas and fish on top of the pasta. Top with the cheese sauce and sprinkle with breadcrumbs. Bake for 25 to 30 minutes, or until golden brown on top. Serve with grated carrots, a side salad, or boiled potatoes.

Norwegian Meatballs
with Brown Sauce, Mushy Peas, Boiled Potatoes, and Lingonberry Jam

Meatballs are Norwegian comfort food at its finest. Literally translated as "meat cakes," Norwegian *kjøttkaker* are closely related to their more popular Swedish cousins, but Norwegian meatballs are larger and flatter. Norwegian meatballs are served with a brown sauce or gravy that is slightly less sweet than the gravy served in Sweden and is not made with heavy cream.

For this recipe, you will need finely ground beef and pork. If these are hard to find where you live, buy the ground meat from your butcher or grocery store and grind more finely at home with a food processor or meat grinder. Also, be sure you fry these meatballs in butter, not oil or margarine. Frying them in butter gives them their distinctive flavor.

I like to serve these hearty meatballs with brown gravy made from the leftover pan fat, boiled potatoes, mushy peas, and cranberry jam. I normally use a store-bought lingonberry jam found in Norway, but you can find comparable substitutes online.

Meatballs and Brown Sauce

Ingredients

Serves 4 to 6

500 grams (~1 pound) pork,
    finely ground
500 grams (~1 pound) beef,
    finely ground
4 teaspoons salt
3 tablespoons potato flour
1/2 teaspoon ground nutmeg
1/4 teaspoon ground ginger
2 eggs
125 milliliters (1/2 cup) milk
Butter for frying
2 tablespoons all-purpose flour
250 milliliters (1 cup) chicken
    stock
Salt and pepper

Directions

In a large bowl, combine the meats, salt, spices, and potato flour. Mix thoroughly with a large spoon or your hands until all ingredients are well incorporated. Add the milk and eggs and combine. Chill the mixture in the refrigerator for 30 minutes.

Use a wet spoon to form the chilled mixture into 6 large or 9 medium balls, then flatten each ball slightly with the back of the spoon.

Melt the butter in a frying pan over medium heat, taking care not to burn. Add the meatballs to the pan, being careful not to crowd them. Fry the meatballs on one side until they are medium brown, then flip them. Brown on the other side, but do not cook the meatballs all the way through. Once the meatballs have browned on both sides, remove from the pan and set aside.

Keeping the pan over medium heat, sprinkle the flour over the pan drippings and whisk to form a smooth, lump-free paste. Add the chicken stock and whisk until incorporated and smooth. Bring the sauce to a boil and cook, whisking continuously, until it reaches your preferred thickness. Season with salt and pepper to taste.

Return the meatballs to the pan, stir into the brown sauce, and cook for 10 minutes. This will cook the meatballs all the way through. Serve with mushy peas (recipe follows), boiled potatoes, and lingonberry jam.

Ertestuing (Mushy Peas)

1 425-gram/15-ounce can
    of peas
1 tablespoon butter
Salt and pepper

Using a hand blender, pulse the peas at low speed until lightly creamed but still somewhat chunky. Transfer peas to a small saucepan, add the butter, and warm thoroughly. Season with salt and pepper to taste.

Poached Salmon

One of the many great things about life in Norway is the abundance of relatively inexpensive but high-quality salmon. Here is one of my favorite ways to cook this healthful, oily fish in a simple but classic way. If you can find wild salmon in your area, use it for this recipe.

Ingredients

Serves 4

1 liter (4 cups) water
1 medium onion, halved
1 teaspoon salt
1 bay leaf
1 tablespoon black peppercorns
4 salmon fillets or steaks
Salt
Freshly ground white pepper

Directions

Combine all ingredients except salmon and bring to a boil for 3 minutes, then decrease to a low simmer.

Season the fish with salt and freshly ground white pepper. Add the fish to the poaching liquid, cover, and poach for 5 to 7 minutes or until the fish turns a pale "salmon" color and flakes easily. Be careful not to overcook the fish! Remove the fish from the pot, drain, and serve.

Fårikål

Every year, the last Thursday in September is celebrated in Norway as Fårikål Day. On this day, *fårikål*, the Norwegian national dish, is eaten en masse all over the country.

Fårikål is a homely one-pot stew containing cabbage, whole black peppercorns, and lamb. Although maybe not the prettiest of dishes, *fårikål* is Norwegian soul food at its coziest.

Ingredients

Serves 6

1 1/2 kilograms (~3 pounds) cabbage, cut into wedges

1 1/2 kilograms (~3 pounds) stewing lamb meat, cut into large chunks

4 teaspoons whole black peppercorns

2 teaspoons salt

300 milliliters (1 1/4 cup) water

Directions

Layer the meat, cabbage, peppercorns, and salt in the bottom of a large pot, pour in the water, and bring to a boil. After the water has come to a boil, decrease the heat to low and simmer until the meat is tender, about 2 to 3 hours. Serve with warm boiled potatoes.

Grilled Leg of Lamb

Grilled leg of lamb has become a popular dish over the last few years in Norway, largely because lamb tends to be more durable (and therefore more forgiving) on the grill. For this method of cooking, I usually marinate the meat for a few hours at room temperature, then shake off the excess before placing it on the grill. This recipe calls for garlic powder, as fresh garlic tends to burn quite easily on the grill and turn bitter—which is a real turn off, to say the least.

Although it's a less traditional method of cooking leg of lamb in Norway, if the weather permits, it's a great way to free up space in the kitchen (for making more cakes, of course!) and enjoy the first few spring weekends with decent weather. Grilled leg of lamb is great for summer gatherings, as well, since this cut of meat is budget-friendly and serves a crowd with minimal fuss. I usually leave my meat on the bone, but feel free to butterfly yours off the bone if you prefer.

Ingredients

Serves 8 to 10

3 shallots

2 tablespoons garlic powder

2 tablespoons fresh rosemary,
 chopped

2 tablespoons apple cider
 vinegar

4 tablespoons olive oil

Kosher salt and freshly ground
 black pepper

1 (~1 1/2-kilogram/
 3 1/3-pound) leg of lamb

Directions

Place all ingredients except the lamb in a blender and blend to create a smooth marinade. Place the leg of lamb in a clean plastic bag, then pour in the marinade and spread it all over both sides of the meat. Close the bag and allow it to sit at room temperature for 2 to 3 hours.

During the last 30 minutes of marinating the lamb, prepare the grill. If using a charcoal grill, prepare the coals so that they form a single layer. You need continuous, even heat to ensure the leg cooks evenly.

Remove the leg of lamb from the marinade and place it, bottom side down, on the grill. Sear one side for 4 to 6 minutes, then flip the leg over and sear the other side for another 4 to 6 minutes. Cover the grill and allow the lamb to cook for an additional 45 to 55 minutes or until a meat thermometer inserted into the thickest part of the leg registers 55° C/130° F.

Once the leg is fully cooked, remove it from the grill and allow it to rest for 10 to 15 minutes. Slice the lamb and serve with potato salad or a side salad.

Komle:
Norwegian Potato Dumplings

Komle goes by many regional names: *klubber, raspeboller*, or simply *boller*. They are slightly salty dumplings, served warm, and made with potatoes—Norway's national vegetable. You will want to use large starchy potatoes instead of the small waxy varieties for this recipe.

I first tried *komle* during my early months in Norway and have been enjoying them ever since. Served with all the accompaniments, *komle* can be quite heavy, which makes it the perfect dish for winter or fall. *Komle* is traditionally served with buttermilk or a pilsner beer.

Accompaniments

Shredded meat from a pork knuckle or ham hock
Cooked sausage
Cooked bacon, cut into bits
Boiled rutabaga
Melted butter

Ingredients

**Makes about 6 large or 8
medium dumplings**

*1 large (500-gram/~1-pound)
pork knuckle or 2 medium
lightly smoked ham hocks*

*2 medium (~170 gram/6 ounces)
starchy potatoes, peeled,
boiled, and mashed*

*6 medium (~500 grams/18
ounces) raw starchy potatoes,
peeled and coarsely grated*

85 grams (2/3 cup) barley flour

*60 grams (1/4 cup) all-purpose
flour*

1 teaspoon salt

*1/2 teaspoon finely ground black
pepper*

Directions

Fill a large pot three-quarters full with water and set on high heat. When the water begins to boil, add the pork knuckle or ham hock and cook at a low or medium simmer for 1 hour. Remove the cooked meat and set it aside to cool. Retain the cooking liquid in the pot; it will be used to cook the dumplings.

Using your hands or a piece of cheesecloth, squeeze the raw, grated potatoes to get rid of as much water as possible. Place the squeezed raw potato in a large bowl, add the remaining ingredients, and mix until well combined. The dough will look very wet at this stage but should clump together easily. If not, add a bit more flour to the dough until it clumps together easily.

With wet hands, shape the dough into 6 small or 8 medium dumplings. If you like, in the center of each dumpling, stuff a small piece of shredded pork from the cooked pork knuckle or ham hock.

Return the cooking liquid to boiling. With a slotted spoon, lower the dumplings into the boiling water one by one. Decrease the heat to a constant simmer. (If the water boils while the dumplings are cooking, they will fall apart.) Simmer for 35 to 40 minutes, until the dumplings float to the surface and are no longer raw in the middle.

Serve the dumplings immediately with the accompaniments and/or some of the cooking broth. If you have leftovers, chill them overnight in the refrigerator. The next day, slice the dumplings into rounds, lightly pan fry in butter or bacon fat, and serve with any of the remaining accompaniments on the side.

Reindeer Steak
with Brown Cheese Sauce

Reindeer meat is popular in Norway and eaten year-round in salamis and other cured forms. Near Christmastime, it is available in supermarkets and is usually prepared in the same manner as venison and other lean game meats. Reindeer meat is quite lean and high in omega-3 fatty acids and vitamin B-12, making it well worth the expense (which can be high depending on where you live). A few producers in Alaska and Canada offer high-quality reindeer meat. In England, reindeer meat is available in specialist boutiques and via mail order.

My version is served with a sauce made from Norwegian brown cheese, locally called *brunost*. *Brunost* was created in the 1850s by milkmaid Anne Hov in Solbråsetra, Gudbrandsdal, Norway, and is made from caramelized whey. The creation of this fudge-like cheese was part accident, part innovative thinking, and was such a success that it ended up saving Anne's farm from financial ruin it. *Brunost* comes in several varieties, with varying percentages of cow's and goat's milk blended together.

Ingredients

Serves 6

750 grams (~1 2/3 pounds)
    reindeer steak
1/2 cup dry red wine
1/2 cup olive oil
6 to 8 juniper berries, crushed
Salt and freshly ground black
    pepper
2 tablespoons butter

Directions

In a large bowl, stir together the wine, olive oil, juniper berries, salt, and pepper. Add the meat and marinate for 20 minutes to 1 hour at room temperature.

Preheat the oven to 200° C/390° F.

Melt the butter in a large frying pan over medium-high. Add the meat and sear on each side for 2 to 3 minutes, until a slight crust begins to form. Transfer the meat to a roasting pan, add a few tablespoons of the marinade, and place the pan in the preheated oven. Roast for 10 minutes.

Decrease the oven heat to 160 C°/320 F° and roast the meat for another 20 minutes. Remove the meat from the oven and allow it to rest, covered, for 10 minutes. After the meat has rested, slice and serve with brown cheese sauce (recipe follows).

Brown Cheese Sauce

2 tablespoons butter
2 tablespoons all-purpose flour
250 milliliters (1 cup) chicken
    or beef stock
300 milliliters (~1 1/4) whipping
    cream
150 grams (~5 1/3 ounces)
    brown cheese (such as Ski
    Queen)
Salt and freshly ground black
    pepper

Slowly melt the butter in a saucepan over medium heat. Just before the butter has completely melted, stir in the flour. Add the stock and cream and stir until smooth. Add the brown cheese and stir until the cheese melts and forms a smooth sauce, about 5 minutes. Season the sauce with salt and pepper to taste, and allow it to simmer over medium-low heat for about 10 minutes, or until thick and smooth.

Cucumber Salad (page 81) and Potato Salad (page 82)

Soups and Side Dishes

Cauliflower Soup

This simple cauliflower recipe is very satisfying and is a great way to get your family to eat more of this very underrated vegetable. I normally sauté my onions in bacon fat, as I keep a jar of it in my refrigerator. Bacon fat is packed full of flavor, and using it here is an easy way to add a lot of flavor to your soup. Butter is a good substitute if bacon fat isn't available.

Ingredients

Serves 4 to 6

1 medium white onion, finely
  chopped
2 tablespoons bacon fat
  or butter
1 medium head of cauliflower,
  cored and coarsely chopped
750 milliliters (3 cups) chicken
  stock
125 milliliters (1/2 cup)
  whipping cream
Salt and pepper to taste
4 tablespoons cooked, chopped
  bacon

Directions

In a large pot over medium heat, sauté the onion in the bacon fat until translucent, being very careful to not burn. Add the cauliflower and stock and bring to a boil. Decrease the heat and simmer for 10 to15 minutes.

Remove the pot from the stove and allow to cool slightly for 10 minutes. Stir in the cream.

Using an immersion blender, puree the contents of the pot until smooth. Season to taste with salt and pepper. Top with chopped, crispy bacon.

Brennsnut

All things considered, *brennsnut* is one of my favorite things to eat when life gets busy, almost too busy to even cook a proper meal—especially in the long, cold months of fall and winter. What I simply adore about *brennsnut* is that it's a hearty stew, guaranteed to warm you to your core, and it won't hurt your wallet either. All of the ingredients are budget-friendly and readily available in most supermarkets. This stew is packed full of root vegetables and nicely uses up any leftover cooked meats. All this goodness swims in a flavorful broth.

If tradition stands true in your kitchen, this recipe should be prepared with homemade lamb stock and lamb meat. However, depending on your location, these ingredients may not be easily available. I've found beef and chicken stock to be reasonable substitutes. Extra meatballs or sausages are both a decent swap for the lamb meat.

Ingredients

Serves 6

750 grams (1 1/2 pounds) cooked meat (any combination of lamb, sausages, or Norwegian-style meatballs)

2 liters (8 1/2 cups) lamb, beef, or chicken stock

4 carrots, peeled and sliced

1 rutabaga, peeled and cubed

8 potatoes, peeled and cubed

1 yellow onion, diced

Salt and pepper to taste

Directions

In a large pot, bring the stock or water to a gentle boil over medium-high heat. When the liquid is boiling, add the vegetables and meat. Decrease the heat and simmer for 25 minutes, or until the vegetables are soft. Season to taste with salt and pepper. Serve with your favorite *flatbrød* (flatbread) or homemade bread.

Lapskaus:
Norwegian Meat and Potato Stew

∞∞

Lapskaus is a hearty Norwegian stew of meat and vegetables. I enjoy *lapskaus* in winter made with lightly cured salted pork, which can be difficult to find outside of Norway. Use stewing pork meat as a substitute if you can't find salted pork in your area.

Ingredients

Serves 4-6

3 tablespoons butter

500 grams (1 pound) pork meat,
    cut into medium-sized cubes

6 potatoes

3 carrots

1 small rutabaga

500 milliliters (2 cups) chicken
    stock or water

Salt and pepper

Directions

Melt the butter in a large, heavy-bottomed pot over medium heat. Brown the cubed pork, working in small batches and removing the cooked pork to a plate, if necessary.

Return all the meat to the pot and pour in the stock or water, then bring to a light boil. Add the vegetables and simmer over medium heat until the meat and vegetables are tender, about 90 minutes. Season to taste with salt and pepper and serve with crispbread.

Cucumber Salad

Cucumber salad is a Norwegian mainstay. My recipe for this classic is made modern with thin strips of cucumber resembling ribbons, instead of the usual chopped cucumber.

Ingredients

Serves 4 to 6

150 milliliters (2/3 cup) white
   vinegar
150 milliliters (2/3 cup) water
3 1/2 tablespoons sugar
1/2 teaspoon salt
1/4 teaspoon ground white
   pepper
2 tablespoons fresh parsley
1 English cucumber (also called
   European cucumbers
   in the U.S.)

Directions

Mix together the vinegar, water, sugar, salt, and white pepper in a small bowl. Set aside. Slice the cucumber lengthwise with a vegetable peeler. You want the strips to be long and thin, like ribbons.

In a large bowl, toss the cucumber with the vinegar mixture. Refrigerate for 30 minutes, then top with parsley and serve.

Norwegian Potato Salad

Norwegians love potatoes, and this is one of the more exciting ways to eat them. Made without sweet pickles and boiled eggs, Norwegian potato salad is very different from the potato salad I grew up eating, but it is delicious nonetheless and is a great alternative if you have guests who do not like eggs or are allergic to them. This potato salad is made very creamy using sour cream, mayonnaise, and milk, providing a rich addition to meals that include salted meats, barbecue, or crispbread.

Ingredients

Serves 4 to 6

8 large starchy potatoes
4 teaspoons salt, divided
250 milliliters (1 cup) sour
    cream
125 milliliters (1/2 cup)
    mayonnaise
125 milliliters (1/2 cup) milk
1/2 teaspoon freshly ground
    black pepper
2 teaspoons sugar
2 tablespoons chopped leek
    stems

Directions

Peel the potatoes and cut into 2 1/2-centimeter/1-inch chunks. Place the potatoes in a medium pot, add 3 teaspoons of the salt, and cover the potatoes with cold water. Boil the potatoes for about 20 minutes, or until they are soft and break apart when pricked with a fork. Drain the potatoes and allow them to cool slightly but not completely.

Mix all remaining ingredients together to form a dressing. Pour the dressing over the top of the potatoes and let the salad stand at room temperature for 15 minutes, so the potatoes absorb some of the dressing. Refrigerate for 2 hours and serve.

Perfect Boiled Potatoes

Boiled potatoes accompany almost every dinnertime meal in Norway. Here is my method for making them perfectly, every time. The secret is not only in the type of potatoes you use, but in starting to boil the water with the potatoes already in the pot.

Ingredients

500 grams (1 pound) potatoes
1 tablespoon salt

Directions

Peel the potatoes and place them in a medium pot. Add the salt and cover with cold water. Bring the water to a boil, and boil the potatoes for about 20 minutes, or until they are soft and break apart when pricked with a fork. Drain the potatoes and allow them to cool completely before serving.

Smoked Salmon Quiche (page 94)

Buns, Pastries, and Tarts

One Dough, Many Buns

Norwegian *boller* (literally, "balls") are a staple in every bakery and cafe in Norway, as well as in most Norwegian households. They are essentially buns made from a sweetened, cardamom-scented dough that has been leavened with yeast. They are much like British hot cross buns, without the cross.

Boller come in several varieties, including round ones with raisins or chocolate. A fancier variety called *skillingsboller* come filled with cinnamon and sugar and resemble North American–style cinnamon buns (sans glaze). Another type of *boller* is the beautifully knotted variety known as *kanelsnurr* ("cinnamon spinner"). *Skoleboller,* or "school balls," are topped with vanilla custard, glaze, and flaked, unsweetened coconut.

These main types of *boller* are popular and beloved—and for good reason. They are great to tuck into when it's gray outside and all you want to do is curl up with a newspaper and a cup of very strong black coffee. They are Norwegian comfort food of the most honest sort.

In Norway, most cooks would probably use fresh yeast, but I've used active dry yeast in this recipe to make it friendly to an international audience. All ingredients must be at room temperature when you begin, including the butter and eggs. While this dough can be made by hand, using a stand mixer will make your life much, much easier.

Basic Boller

Ingredients

Makes 10 to 15 buns

300 milliliters (1 1/4 cups) milk

*1 package (7 grams/1/4 ounce)
    dry, active yeast*

*500 grams (1 pound) all-purpose
    flour*

1 teaspoon salt

1 teaspoon ground cardamom

75 grams (1/3 cups) sugar

1 egg, beaten

*75 grams (1/3 cup) butter,
    melted*

Directions

Heat the milk until slightly warm (but not hot). Pour half to the milk into the bowl of your mixer and add the yeast. Allow the yeast to proof for 5 minutes, then add the remaining dry ingredients. Using the dough hook, mix on medium speed to form a dough. Add the egg and mix to incorporate. Slowly add the rest of the warm milk to the dough and mix at low speed for 5 to 7 minutes.

When the dough sticks to the hook and pulls away from the sides of the bowl completely, add one third of the melted butter. Continue mixing to incorporate, and repeat twice until the remaining butter is thoroughly incorporated. Cover the bowl with a tea towel or plastic wrap/cling film and set aside to rise for 45 to 60 minutes, or until the dough has doubled in size.

Preheat the oven to 200° C/390° F. Line a baking sheet with parchment paper and set aside.

Once the dough has risen, punch it down, then knead it by hand on a floured surface until it is soft and no longer sticky. Shape the dough balls. Place the balls on a parchment paper–lined baking sheet and allow to rise again for 15 to 30 minutes. After the buns have risen, brush the top of each with beaten egg. Bake for 10 to 15 minutes, or until light golden brown.

Basic Variations

To make boller with raisins, soak 250 grams (1 2/3 cups) raisins in water for 1 hour. Drain the raisins and mix in before you add the butter to the dough.

To make boller with chocolate, before you add the butter to the dough, mix in 250 milliliters (1 cup) semisweet mini-chocolate chips.

Skillingsboller

Ingredients

Filling

55 grams (1/4 cup) butter
  (at room temperature)
3 tablespoons ground cinnamon
50 grams (1/4 cup) sugar
Pearl sugar or demerara sugar,
  for topping

Directions

To make fancier *skillingsboller,* follow the original *boller* recipe (page 86) through preheating the oven and lining the baking sheet with parchment paper.

Once the dough has risen, knead it on a lightly floured surface for approximately 5 to 7 minutes. The dough will feel slightly oily at first. Roll the dough into a large, flat circle.

In a small bowl, stir the butter, cinnamon, and sugar together to form a paste. Spread the cinnamon paste onto the large flat circular form and, beginning at one edge, roll the dough into a log. Slice the log into rounds about 1 1/4 centimeters or half an inch thick and place on the baking sheet. Allow the rounds to rise for another 15 minutes, brush with beaten egg, and sprinkle with pearl sugar or demerara sugar. Bake for 10 to 15 minutes, or until light golden brown.

Kanelsnurr

Ingredients

Filling

115 grams (1/2 cup) butter,
    softened
6 tablespoons ground cinnamon
75 grams (1/3 cup) sugar

Directions

To make super fancy Norwegian cinnamon buns, known
as *kanelsnurr* (cinnamon spinner), follow the original *boller*
recipe (page 86) through preheating the oven and lining
the baking sheet with parchment paper.

While the dough is rising, mix the butter, cinnamon, and
sugar to form a soft paste. Set aside. Once the dough has risen,
knead the dough on a lightly floured surface for approximately
5 to 7 minutes. The dough will feel slightly oily to begin with.
Roll out the dough into a large, flat circle. Spread the cinnamon
paste on half the circle. Fold the opposite half of the circle on
top of the filling and cut into strips that are 2 1/2 centimeters
(1 inch) wide.

To create the classic twisted shape, twist the strand, then tie
it into a knot. Transfer all the cinnamon buns to the baking
sheet and allow to rise for an additional 15 minutes. After
the buns have risen, brush with beaten egg and bake for
15 minutes, or until light golden brown.

Skoleboller

For *skoleboller,* you'll want to make the custard first, then allow it to cool before making the dough and finally assembling the buns. Make sure the coconut is unsweetened, or the buns will be overwhelmingly sweet.

Ingredients

Topping
1 egg, beaten
4 to 6 tablespoons flaked,
    unsweetened coconut

Vanilla Custard
400 milliliters (1 1/3 cups) milk
1 vanilla bean
6 egg yolks
50 grams (1/4 cup) sugar

Glaze
25 grams (1/4 cup) powdered
    sugar
2 tablespoons milk

Directions

In a small pot, warm the milk gently over medium heat until warm but not hot. Split the vanilla bean in half lengthwise and scrape the seeds into the milk.

In a medium bowl, whisk together the egg yolks, sugar, and cornstarch. Gradually ladle the warm milk into the egg mixture, whisking the milk into the eggs. Once you have incorporated all of the milk, return the milk mixture to the pot.

Over medium-low heat, bring the mixture to a low simmer, whisking constantly. Be careful not to bring the milk to a boil as it will curdle and you will need to begin all over again.

Once the custard begins to thicken, decrease the heat and continue to whisk until it is thick enough to coat the back of a spoon without running. Take the pan off the heat and transfer the custard to a heat-resistant bowl. Set aside and allow the custard to cool completely.

To make the *skoleboller*, follow the original *boller* recipe (page 86) through preheating the oven and lining the baking sheet with parchment paper. Once the dough has risen, knead on a lightly floured surface for approximately 5 to 7 minutes. The dough will feel slightly oily to begin with but will become less so as it is kneaded.

Next, roll the dough into a log, cut into 10 to 15 pieces, then shape the pieces into balls. Place the balls on the baking sheet and allow to rise for 15 minutes. Once the balls have risen, flatten them slightly so they look like puffy discs. Press your thumb into the middle of each disc to make a well, then fill the well with the custard. Brush the area surrounding the well with a bit of beaten egg, then bake for 10 to 15 minutes. Cool the *skoleboller* on a wire rack for about 10 minutes, or until cool enough to handle.

Once the *boller* have cooled, stir together the powdered sugar and milk to make a smooth glaze. Drizzle the glaze over the top of the sides of the *skoleboller* (not over the custard in the center, however), then dip the tops into the flaked coconut. This will give the *skoleboller* their signature look.

Solskinnskringle

Solskinnskringle is another classic, custard-filled Norwegian pastry and is usually served with strong black coffee. This is one of my favorite "coffee and cake" pastries to serve; it's perfect for the next time you have family or friends coming around. That said, be sure you set aside a few hours to ensure the *boller* dough has time to complete the extra rising. The payoff is spectacular— and well worth it if you'd like to wow your guests or family. You'll want to make the vanilla custard first, then prepare the dough and assemble the *kringle*.

Ingredients

Filling

55 grams (1/4 cup) butter,
    at room temperature
3 tablespoons ground cinnamon
50 grams (1/4 cup) sugar

Glaze

25 grams (1/4 cup) powdered
    sugar
2 tablespoons milk

Directions

Prepare the vanilla custard (page 90) and set aside to cool. Next, follow the original *boller* recipe (page 86) through pre-heating the oven and lining the baking sheet with parchment paper. Once the dough has risen, knead for approximately 5 to 7 minutes on a lightly floured surface.

After kneading, roll a piece of dough into a small ball and set aside. Roll out the remaining dough into a large, flat circle.

In a small bowl, stir together the butter, cinnamon, and sugar to form a paste. Spread the cinnamon paste evenly over the circle of dough. Beginning at one edge, roll the dough into a log.

Flatten the small ball of dough into a 7 1/2--centimeter/3-inch circle. Shape the log of dough around the small circle, press the ends together to form a ring, and press gently to attach the ring to the circle. Using a knife or sharp scissors and working at a slight angle, make a series of 7 or 9 cuts in the dough ring, making sure to cut only about two-thirds of the way through the ring. The dough ring will now have 8 or 10 segments. Gently tug one segment in toward the center of the ring, and tug the next segment outward. Repeat until all segments have been separated and the ring somewhat resembles a flower.

Transfer the *kringle* to the baking sheet and allow to rise for an additional 25 to 30 minutes. Brush the *kringle* with beaten egg, fill the center with vanilla custard, and bake for 30 to 40 minutes, or until light golden brown.

While the *kringle* is baking, stir together the powdered sugar and milk to form a smooth glaze. Cool the pastry for 10 minutes, then drizzle with the glaze.

Plum and Cherry Crumble

Much of the fruit in Norway is grown in the Hardanger region. The fresh cherries and plums that are sold in supermarkets and at the roadside in summer make this crumble the perfect dessert to serve alongside vanilla ice cream. I've used almond flour in this recipe to add depth, while the cinnamon, cherry, and almond flavors go together quite nicely in this crumble.

Ingredients

Serves 6 to 8

Fruit Mixture
250 grams (1/2 pound) plums,
    pitted and cut into eighths
250 grams (1/2 pound) Morello
    cherries, pitted and halved
3 tablespoons sugar
3 tablespoons all-purpose flour
1/4 teaspoon ground cinnamon
Pinch of salt

Crumb Topping
60 grams (1/4 cup) unsalted
    butter, cut into small pieces
120 grams (1 cup) all-purpose
    flour
60 grams (1/2 cup) almond flour
130 grams (2/3 cup) sugar
1 teaspoon baking powder
1/4 teaspoon salt

Directions

Preheat the oven to 190° C/375° F.

In a large bowl, combine all the fruit mixture ingredients. Spread the mixture in the bottom of an ungreased baking dish and set aside.

In another large bowl, combine the all the crumb topping ingredients. Using your hands, mix until the ingredients are well combined and the mixture resembles sand.

Top the fruit mixture with the crumb mixture and bake for 30 to 35 minutes, or until the top is browned and the fruit is bubbling. Cool for 15 to 30 minutes before serving. Serve with vanilla ice cream.

Smoked Salmon Quiche

I've used frozen puff pastry for the crust on this quiche, but feel free to use a short-crust pastry if you prefer. Puff pastry is widely available, which is wonderful, but the size of puff pastry sheets tends to vary by producer. Make sure you thaw enough puff pastry to cover the bottom and sides of your baking dish.

Ingredients

Serves 6 to 8

2 to 3 sheets frozen puff pastry, thawed

6 eggs

225 milliliters (1 cup) heavy cream

100 grams (3.5 ounces) smoked salmon, chopped into large pieces

1 tablespoon fresh dill

2 tablespoons chopped leeks

1/2 teaspoon salt

1/2 teaspoon freshly ground black pepper

Directions

Preheat the oven to 200° C/400° F.

Roll out the puff pastry into a circle and press it into the bottom and up the sides of a large tart pan. Pierce the bottom of the pastry several times with a fork. Bake for 7 to 10 minutes, then remove it from the oven and set aside. The pastry should have turned a slight golden brown and should look flaky.

Whisk together the eggs, cream, dill, leeks, salt, and pepper in a large bowl. Pour the egg mixture into the puff pastry and top with smoked salmon. Return the quiche to the oven and bake for 20 to 25 minutes, or until it is firm in the center. Allow the quiche to rest for 10 minutes before serving.

Bløtkake (page 102)

Cakes and Desserts

Stewed Prunes with Cream

Stewed prunes served with cream is a traditional Norwegian dessert beloved by small and big Vikings alike. In the U.S., prunes have a tarnished reputation for being boring, tasteless, and used only for digestive troubles. I've come to enjoy this lovely Norwegian dessert, which highlights how flavorful prunes are and how the best treats are often the simplest. Normally this dessert is thickened with potato flour, but I've left it out with good results.

Ingredients

Serves 4

12 prunes
50 grams (1/4 cup) sugar
100 milliliters (~7 tablespoons) honey
2 teaspoons lemon juice
125 milliliters (1/2 cup) water
Whipping cream

Directions

In a medium pot over medium-low heat, simmer all ingredients except cream until the prunes have swollen and roughly doubled in size. Some of the prunes might break open; this is normal.

Once the prunes have doubled in size, turn off the heat and cover the pot. Allow the prunes to cool until just slightly warm, about 20 minutes. Serve topped with cream.

Rhubarb Compote

Rhubarb is grown in many Norwegian gardens in spring and is rumored to be best before Midsummer, the longest day of the year, which falls in mid-June. I can't say I've seen many Norwegians buying *rabarbra,* as the locals call it, because most people grow it in their gardens. It is given to friends and family as a housewarming gift or as a friendly gesture.

I serve this with a touch of cream from time to time, but usually as a topping on homemade vanilla ice cream.

Ingredients

Makes 500 milliliters/2 cups

2 pounds fresh rhubarb, roughly chopped
1/2 cup water
3/4 cup granulated sugar
Zest of half a lemon or orange
1/2 teaspoon vanilla bean paste (or 1/2 teaspoon vanilla extract)

Directions

In a large pot, combine all ingredients except vanilla bean paste (or vanilla extract). Simmer over medium-high heat, stirring occasionally, until rhubarb breaks down completely. Remove from heat, stir in the vanilla bean paste (or extract), and allow to cool to room temperature. Serve warm or chilled.

Mini Meringues

It took me a long time to fall in love with meringues. And by a long time, I mean 32 years. The first time I made meringues from scratch, though, all of my previous ill feelings towards them went out the window. I finally figured out what makes meringues so amazing: They look so soft and pillow-like, but taking a bite out of one reveals they are crisp, fragile, and a little bit gooey.

I love this recipe because it is really simple to make (especially if you have a stand mixer), can be made ahead, and is very inexpensive to make for a dinner-party crowd. It's one of those desserts that make you look like a pro to all of your guests, without all that slaving in the kitchen. Top yours with vanilla custard, whipped cream, fresh berries, chocolate shavings, or even a little jam (or some combination thereof).

Ingredients

Makes 8 meringues

*3 egg whites, at room
   temperature*
1/2 teaspoon lemon juice
150 grams (3/4 cup) sugar

Directions

Preheat the oven to 110° C/230° F.

In the bowl of a stand mixer (or large mixing bowl if you are using a hand mixer) whisk the egg whites with the lemon juice until the egg whites double in size and form soft peaks. Continue whisking, adding the sugar 1 tablespoon at a time and incorporating it completely before adding more. After you have added in all of the sugar, keep whisking until the egg whites are glossy.

Line a large baking sheet with parchment paper. Spoon the egg white mixture into a large piping bag (or a zip-top plastic bag with one corner snipped off) and pipe onto the parchment paper.

Bake for 2 hours. When the meringues are finished, they will have a crisp exterior and will lift easily off the paper. Allow to cool completely on a wire rack and serve plain or topped with vanilla custard sauce (recipe follows) and fruit.

Vanilla Custard Sauce

Ingredients

1 vanilla bean
400 milliliters (1 1/3 cup) milk
6 egg yolks
50 grams (1/4 cup) sugar
125 milliliters (1/2) whipping
   cream

Directions

In a medium pot, warm the milk gently over medium heat, until warm but not hot. Split the vanilla bean in half lengthwise and scrape the seeds into the warm milk.

In a large bowl, whisk together the egg yolks, sugar, and cornstarch. Gradually ladle the milk into the egg mixture, whisking it into the eggs. After you have incorporated all the milk, pour the mixture into the pot. Over medium-low heat, bring the milk mixture to a low simmer, whisking continuously. Be careful not to bring to a boil, as it will curdle and you will need to begin all over again. Once the mixture begins to thicken, decrease the heat and continue to whisk until the custard is thick enough to coat the back of a spoon without running. Stir in the cream.

Transfer the custard to a heat-resistant bowl and allow it to cool completely, then pour over the meringues.

Bløtkake

Syttende Mai holds a very special place in my heart, not only because of the fabulous cakes—like this classic *bløtkake*—the beautiful *bunads*, and the cute kids marching with their school bands, but because Syttende Mai is the one day a year modesty goes out the window and it is completely OK to be proud to be Norwegian. I love Norway, and the events on May 17th always give me goosebumps.

Whether you bake it for Syttende Mai or another happy occasion, the keys to making a good *bløtkake* are good sponge cake, fresh fruit, and real whipped cream. My American brothers and sisters: Do not—I repeat, DO NOT—use any of those other white "whipped toppings." Norwegians value this cake for its simplicity and balance—two words not associated with all of those whipped cream–like toppings we have back home in the U.S. You must use real whipped cream for this recipe.

Also, this cake shouldn't be too sweet, too tart, or overwhelmingly heavy. The tartness from the raspberry jam balances out all the whipped cream, and the sponge cake provides structure but is softened by the moistness of the jam. Again, balance is the name of the game here. For this recipe, I've used raspberry jam and whipped cream between the layers of cake, but you can also try using vanilla custard and fresh berries for variation. This cake can (and probably should) be made a day in advance so the jam and cream fillings have time to soak into the cake layers.

If you don't have the chance to join a Syttende Mai parade (or even if you do), make this cake and taste a little piece of Norway!

Thanks *for the* Food

Sponge Cake

Ingredients

Serves 12

*3 large eggs, separated, at room
temperature*
*190 grams (1 1/2 cup) sugar,
divided into three portions*
*290 grams (2 1/4 cups)
all-purpose flour*
3 teaspoons baking powder
1 teaspoon salt
*50 milliliters (1/3 cup plus 1
tablespoon) vegetable oil*
250 milliliters (1 cup) milk
1 1/2 teaspoons vanilla extract

Filling

*900 milliliters (3 3/4 cups)
whipping cream*
*30 grams (2 tablespoons) vanilla
sugar*
*100 grams (3/4 cup) raspberry
jam*
*300 grams (2 to 3 cups) fresh
fruit, sliced (or whole if using
berries)*
*1 recipe vanilla custard sauce
(page 101)*

Directions

Preheat the oven to 180° C/350° F. Grease a 23-centimeter (9-inch) round springform pan and set aside.

In a large bowl and using a hand mixer (or in your stand mixer and using the whisk attachment), beat the egg whites until foamy. Using one of the three portions of sugar, add 2 tablespoons of sugar and continue to whisk. Every 30 seconds, add another 2 tablespoons of sugar until the entire portion has been incorporated and the egg whites are stiff and glossy. Set aside.

In large bowl, sift together the flour and baking powder, then add the remaining two portions of sugar and the salt. Whisk the oil and vanilla plus half the milk into the flour mixture. Add the remaining milk and the egg yolks and continue to whisk for 1 minute, until well combined. Gently fold in the egg whites.

Spread the batter in the prepared springform pan. Bake until a toothpick inserted in the center of the cake comes out clean, about 30 to 40 minutes.

Cool the cake on a wire rack for 15 to 20 minutes, then remove from the pan and allow to cool completely. Once the cake has cooled, use a long, serrated knife to slice it horizontally into three layers. Transfer each layer a separate plate.

Spread the first layer with vanilla custard sauce, then jam, then whipped cream. Position the second layer of cake atop the first and again spread with vanilla custard sauce, jam, and whipped cream. (You really want to apply a good layer of cream between each layer of cake, and be generous with the vanilla custard as the sponge cake will soak it up. Not too generous, but don't skimp.)

Position the third layer on top of the cake, then frost the top and sides of the cake with the remaining whipped cream. Decorate the cake with the berries and fresh fruit. Keep the cake refrigerated until ready to serve, or overnight if possible.

Blueberry-Cheesecake Frozen Yogurt

Not only are blueberries a "superfood" and extremely healthful, they grow wild in Norway during the late summer months and taste like little balls of sweet-tart heaven.

Frozen yogurt tends to get a bad rap, but this recipe uses whole-milk Turkish yogurt and ingredients you can actually pronounce. No mono-modified syrups here, just yogurt with sugar, fruit, and cookie crumbs. Feel free to use gluten-free cookies if you fancy, or goat's milk yogurt for a lactose-reduced option. I advise against using fat-free or low-fat yogurt for this recipe, as the higher water content in the yogurt will increase the potential for ice crystals to form and make the yogurt hard instead of soft and creamy.

Ingredients

Serves 8

1 liter (34 ounces) thick, natural, unflavored yogurt (full-fat Turkish, Greek, or drained)

100 grams (1/2 cup) vanilla sugar (or substitute regular sugar plus the seeds scraped from one vanilla bean)

1 deciliter (2 cups) frozen blueberries

2 deciliter (1 cup) cookie crumbs

Directions

In a medium bowl, combine the yogurt and vanilla sugar. Stir until well combined. Following the instructions of your ice cream maker, add the yogurt mixture to the machine and churn until the yogurt is set. (In my machine, this normally takes about 25 minutes.) Spoon the yogurt into your storage container and stir in the blueberries and cookie crumbs. Freeze the yogurt until hard, about 4 hours. Serve and enjoy!

Thanks *for the* Food

Trollkrem

Trollkrem, or "troll cream," is a great Norwegian dairy-free dessert to serve at your next dinner party.

Ingredients

Serves 12

2 egg whites
125 milliliters (1/2 cup)
    lingonberry jam
50 grams (1/4 cup) vanilla sugar
Lemon balm leaves (optional)

Directions

Using a hand or stand mixer, whisk the egg whites, jam, and vanilla sugar into a thick foam. Garnish with lemon balm leaves and serve.

Tilslørte Bondepiker

Tilslørte bondepiker, translated as "veiled peasant girls" in English, is a classic and quite commonly enjoyed Norwegian dessert. It is served year-round, although slightly more often during the colder months of the year. This traditional dessert makes use of three main ingredients always on hand in most Norwegian kitchens: whipping cream, apples, and breadcrumbs. I love this layered trifle dessert because it's simple to assemble and budget-friendly. Serve in a glass bowl or individual glass dessert dishes to show off each layer of the dessert.

For this recipe, I use a batch of my homemade (unspiced) applesauce when I have it on hand, or the jarred kind when I don't. Instead of the traditional white breadcrumbs, some Norwegian cooks use crumbled digestive biscuits or another crumbled plain cookie and cut back correspondingly on the sugar in the breadcrumb mix. No matter which type of crumbs you use, make sure they are finely crumbled into small bits. Also, feel free to ease up on the cream and add more breadcrumbs to make this dessert more waistline-friendly.

Ingredients

Serves 10

3 teaspoons butter
3 to 4 deciliters (2 1/2 to 3 cups) dry white breadcrumbs
3 teaspoons vanilla sugar
1/2 teaspoon ground cinnamon
300 milliliters (1 1/4 cup) whipping cream
4 3/4 deciliters (2 cups) applesauce
Lemon balm leaves (optional)

Directions

In a medium pan, melt butter over low heat. Remove from heat, add the breadcrumbs, sugar, and cinnamon, and stir until well combined. Scoop the breadcrumb mixture into a heat-proof bowl and set aside to cool. Using a stand mixer or hand mixer, whip cream until stiff peaks form. Set aside.

Spoon a layer of breadcrumbs into the bottom of your serving dish, then a layer of cream, and finally a layer of applesauce. Continue layering until serving dish is full. Garnish with lemon balm leaves and serve.

Thanks *for the* Food

Tilslørte bondepiker

Norwegian Waffles (page 114)

Snacks & Drinks

Potato Lefse

Lefse is to the Norwegian food tradition what corn tortillas are to Mexican cuisine or cornbread to American soul food: part food delivery vessel, part meal accompaniment, and substantive enough to make a meal on its own. There are countless recipes for *lefse* out there, and I've heard some say every family has their own recipe, handed down for hundreds of years. There are the purists who argue against eggs, cream, or sugar in the dough, and those who wouldn't dare make *lefse* without them. I've had *lefse* with eggs and without, with potato and without, all equally good for different reasons.

For first timers, potato *lefse* is a lot less intimidating than thin or thick *lefse*, because the dough is far more forgiving. Ultimately, the amount of flour you will need for this depends on the hardness of the water in your area and how finely milled your flour is, but the following measurements give you a good place to begin. Just "listen to" your dough as you go along, and you should be able to it just right.

While you want to make sure you get your *lefse* as thin as possible—nearly transparent when held up to a sunny window, and with no breaks or holes—be sure not to overwork the gluten through excessive handling. I find using a "sweeping" roll-out method works best. Begin the rolling motion before you reach the edge of the dough, and sweep across and off the dough in a long, continuous movement. (The workout you get from rolling out these beauties will make up for all the butter and sugar you smear on the inside.)

Be sure to cook the *lefse* just until the dough begins to get those lovely tan-to-brown spots, as they will continue to cook slightly after you take them out of the pan. *Lefse* freeze well, so feel free to freeze any leftovers or make a double batch.

Ingredients

Makes 10 to 12 medium lefse

*500 grams (1 pound) starchy,
all-purpose potatoes, peeled
and quartered*

*60 grams (1/4 cup) unsalted
butter, melted and cooled*

*60 milliliters (1/4 cup) heavy
cream*

3 1/2 teaspoons salt, divided

*120 to 180 grams (1 to 1 1/2
cups) all-purpose flour,
divided*

Directions

Place the potatoes in a medium pot, add 1 tablespoon of the salt, and cover with cold water. Bring the water to a boil, and boil the potatoes for about 20 minutes, or until they are soft and break apart when pricked with a fork. Drain the potatoes, set aside, and allow them to cool completely.

Over a large bowl, pass the cooled potatoes through a potato ricer twice to ensure there are absolutely no lumps in the mash. If you do not have a potato ricer, use a potato masher or the back of a fork to mash the potatoes completely. Remember, you want no chunks or clumps. Add the butter, cream, and salt to the mash and stir until completely combined. Refrigerate overnight, or for at least 8 hours.

After the potato mash has chilled, add 120 grams (1 cup) of the flour and stir to thoroughly combine. The resulting dough should clump together quite easily and not be sticky. If your dough is sticky, add more flour, up to 60 grams (1/2 cup).

Knead the dough on a lightly floured surface for 2 to 3 minutes. Divide the dough into 10 to12 equal portions, then roll one portion between your hands to form a ball. (Cover the other dough balls with a tea towel so they don't dry out.) Using a rolling pin on a floured surface, roll the ball into a very thin disc. You want to get your *lefse* as thin as possible without breaking it apart.

Warm a cast iron skillet, crepe pan, pancake pan, or griddle over medium-high heat. Carefully transfer 1 *lefse* to the hot pan and cook until tan spots appear. Roll out another *lefse* and repeat.

Stack your *lefse* on a plate as they come out of the pan, and cover the stack with a tea towel to keep them from drying out. When half of your dough has been cooked, flip the entire stack over to allow the heat from the most recently cooked *lefse* to help keep the older ones soft, then re-cover with the tea towel.

To serve, smear the inside of each *lefse* with butter, sprinkle with sugar, and roll it up. If you are feeding a crowd, slice the *lefse* rolls into bite-sized pieces before serving.

 Thanks for the Food

Thin Lefse

These extra-thin *lefse* are made without potatoes and include cream and milk to help keep the dough pliable and soft before cooking.

Ingredients

Makes 15 to18 medium lefse

1 1/2 kilograms (~12 1/2 cups)
   all-purpose flour
400 grams (2 cups) sugar
2 eggs
300 milliliters (1 1/4 cup)
   whipping cream
500 milliliters (2 cups) milk
2 teaspoons baking powder

Directions

Beat the eggs and sugar together until well incorporated and fluffy. Next, mix in the cream and milk. In a separate bowl, combine the flour and baking power. Stir the flour mixture into the egg mixture to form a dough.

Divide the dough into 15 to 18 equal portions, then roll each portion between your hands to form a ball. Using a rolling pin on a floured surface, roll 1 ball into a very thin disc. (Cover the other dough balls with a tea towel so they don't dry out.) You want to get your *lefse* as thin as possible without breaking it apart.

To cook the *lefse*, warm a cast iron skillet, crepe pan, pancake pan, or griddle over medium-high heat. Carefully transfer 1 *lefse* to the hot pan and cook it until tan spots appear. Roll out another *lefse* and repeat.

Stack your *lefse* on a plate as they come out of the pan, and cover the stack with a tea towel to keep the *lefse* from drying out. When half of your dough has been cooked, flip the entire stack over to allow the heat from the most recently cooked *lefse* to help keep the older ones soft. Be sure to cover the entire stack with a tea towel to keep the *lefse* from drying out.

To serve, smear the inside of your *lefse* with butter, sprinkle with sugar, roll it up, and enjoy. If you are feeding a crowd, try cutting the *lefse* roll into smaller pieces before serving.

Anne's Sveler

Sveler resemble American-style pancakes in preparation method but aren't usually eaten for breakfast like their American cousins. In Norway, we eat these between meals or as a snack along with strong coffee. They are typically topped with brown cheese.

My boyfriend's mother swears by this recipe. It calls for *hjortetakksalt* (baking ammonia), which can be found online outside Norway and in just about every grocery store in Scandinavia. These *sveler* are filled with a lot of love and almost as much butter—which makes them addictive. You have been warned.

Ingredients

Makes 20 sveler

100 grams (1/2 cup) sugar
2 eggs
1 teaspoon hjortetakksalt
1/2 teaspoon baking soda
500 milliliters (2 cups)
    full-fat buttermilk
300 grams (2 1/2 cups)
    all-purpose flour
60 grams (1/4 cup) butter,
    melted

Directions

Using a stand mixer, whip the sugar and eggs together until fluffy and pale. Alternate stirring in the flour and buttermilk until both are well incorporated into the mixture. Add the melted butter and continue to stir until the batter is smooth. Allow the batter to rest for 5 minutes.

For each *sveler,* ladle 63 milliliters (1/4 cup) of batter onto a warm griddle or pan, and cook over medium-high heat for 2 to 3 minutes on each side, until both sides are golden brown. Serve plain or with brown cheese, jam, and sour cream.

Norwegian Waffles

The most famous waffle recipe comes from the Norwegian Seaman's Church—and is one of the things they are loved for the world over, in addition to the many marriages they perform for Norwegians living abroad. This recipe differs from theirs a bit, but I like it anyway.

Waffles in the U.S. are normally eaten for breakfast, but in Norway they are eaten for snacks and between meals. And unlike Belgian- or American-style waffles, Norwegain waffles are usually heart-shaped as well as soft and pliable, making them easy to fold around brown cheese or sour cream and jam. If you can get your hands on a heart-shaped waffle iron outside of Scandinavia (via Amazon or another online seller), be sure to buy one. They are broader and shallower than the ones used in the U.S. and make for more authentic Norwegian waffles.

The secret to a good waffle is to really whip the eggs and sugar together until they are a pale yellow and the eggs are quite aerated. You'll also want to give the dough time to rest before you cook the batter; this allows the gluten strands to form, making for a waffle that is airy but strong enough not to break when you fold it. Your first waffle might come out a bit wonky, but the second will likely be perfect.

Serve your waffles warm or cold and topped with cold, full-fat sour cream, sliced Norwegian brown cheese, strawberry jam, or fruit compote.

Ingredients

Makes 8 to 10 waffles

6 eggs
100 grams (1/2 cup) sugar
1 teaspoon freshly ground
    cardamom
180 ground (1 1/2) cup
    all-purpose flour
1 teaspoon baking powder
Pinch of salt
250 grams (1 cup) sour cream
120 grams (1/2 cup) butter,
    melted
Non-stick cooking spray or
    melted butter for cooking

Directions

Using a stand mixer or a hand mixer, whip the eggs, sugar, and cardamom together until the mixture is quite aerated and turns pale yellow. In a separate bowl, combine the flour, baking powder, and salt. Set aside.

Mix the sour cream and butter into the egg mixture, then add in the dry ingredients. Allow the batter to rest for 20 minutes at room temperature. (Do not skip this step.)

Five minutes before the end of the resting period, preheat your waffle iron. When the iron is hot, spray with cooking spray or brush with melted butter and pour the batter into the iron, taking care not to over- or under-fill the waffle iron. Cook the waffle until slightly brown, then remove from the iron and serve.

Pjalt

I first discovered these lovely treats in summer 2014 while on a "food safari," a 5-hour minibus-driven tasting tour of food-producing farms in the Røros area of Norway. At each stop along the tour, we were able to meet the farmers or producers responsible for the foods we tasted, and heard their family stories and historical anecdotes about the foods produced in the Røros region.

Our last stop on the tour was at Kalsa Gårdsbakeri for coffee—which in Norway means not just coffee but some type of sweet treat will be served. The sweet treat end-up being *lemse* (similar to *lefse*) and *pjalt*, which resemble American pancakes (although prepared completely differently). I fell in love with both treats at first bite.

Pjalt are akin to *sveler*, essentially flatbread leavened with some combination of *hjortetakksalt* (baking ammonia, formerly made with powdered deer antler), baking powder, and the very thick, acidic milk product unique to Røros call *tjukkmjølk* (literally "thick milk"). Kefir (usually found in stores stocking foods from eastern Europe or Russia) or full-fat buttermilk can be substituted for *tjukkmjølk* in this recipe.

Ingredients

Makes 12 to 14 pjalt

1 kilogram (2 pounds)
  all-purpose flour
250 grams (1 1/4 cup) sugar
2 tablespoons hjortetakksalt
2 tablespoons baking soda
2 tablespoons baking powder
250 grams (1 cup) butter, chilled
1 liter (4 1/4 cups) tjukkmjølk
  (full-fat kefir or buttermilk
  also work well)

Directions

Combine all ingredients except the butter and *tjukkmjølk* (or kefir/buttermilk, if substituting). Add the butter, and crumble the mixture together in your hands until it resembles sand. Gradually add the *tjukkmjølk* (or substitute) and mix together until a smooth dough forms.

Divide the dough into 2 portions. On a generously floured surface, roll out one portion at a time until it is 3 millimeters or 1/8 inch thick.

Once you've rolled the dough out flat, use a round cookie cutter or the rim of a drinking glass to cut circles out of the dough. Cook the *pjalt* dough on a griddle or pan over medium-high heat for 3 to 4 minutes on each side, or until light brown. Served topped with brown cheese.

Red Currant Saft

Saft is more or less a juice concentrate, and not so long ago was an extremely important food product for most Norwegians. For many, it served as their primary source of vitamin C and trace minerals during the long and dark winters most of the country experiences every year.

Most Norwegians exclusively use cheesecloth strainers to make saft, but I like to use a fine mesh strainer to begin with, then run the saft through a cheesecloth strainer a second time catch any seeds or skins that may have passed through the first time.

If you can't find fresh red currants in your area, use raspberries instead.

Ingredients

Makes 750 ml (~3 cups)

1 kilogram (2 pounds) fresh red
    currants
500 milliliters (2 cups) water
300 grams (1 1/2 cups) sugar

Directions

Wash the currants and place them in a large pot. Add the water and boil for 5 minutes. Using a fine sieve, strain the mixture. Strain a second time using cheesecloth laid in the sieve to be sure you've removed seeds, skins, and anything else from the juice.

Stir in the sugar. Boil the juice for 10 to 15 minutes or until no foam remains on the surface. Pour the saft into a clean glass bottle with a lid. To serve, mix one part saft with one part cold water. Store leftover saft in the refrigerator.

Snarøl

Snarøl, or "quick beer," is a beverage made from an alcohol-free malt drink called *vørterøl* plus sugar, fresh yeast, and lemon. It is drunk near Christmas time, but I tend to drink it anytime a craving hits. *Vørterøl*, which gives the *snarøl* its unique taste, is high in B vitamins, giving this drink its health-promoting properties. It's likely that *vørterøl* is a mainstay from the days when Norway and Denmark were one country, as the world's largest producer of *vørterøl* is in Denmark.

Most African, Caribbean, and South American groceries carry *vørterøl*, or another alcohol- and caffeine-free malted beverage, under various brand names.

Ingredients

Makes 3 liters (~6 1/3 pints)

3 liters (~3 quarts plus 2/3 cup)
    water
250 grams (1 1/4 cups) sugar
Juice of 1/2 a lemon
250 milliliters (1 cup) vørterøl
    (or any alcohol- and
    caffeine-free malted
    beverage)
1 teaspoon fresh yeast

Directions

Stir together the water, sugar, and lemon juice in a large pot and bring to a boil. When the water begins to boil, remove from the heat and allow to cool for 1 hour. Add the *vørterøl* and yeast, stirring well until the yeast dissolves. Allow the liquid to sit at room temperature for 8 hours, or overnight. (The longer the *snarøl* sits, the more strongly carbonated it will become due to the yeast activity.) Serve chilled and store the finished *snarøl* in the refrigerator.

Krumkaker (page 126)

Christmastime Dishes and Treats

Medisterkaker with Sauerkraut

Norwegians love Christmas, and these "meat cakes" or meatballs have been served on pretty much every traditional Christmas dinner table at which I've ever been a guest.

In Norway, one can buy *medisterdeig*, ground pork with a fat content of around 25%, in most stores. If you live outside Norway and have access to a good butcher, ask them to grind pork for you with some extra fat added to it for a really authentic-tasting meatball. Otherwise, aim to buy the fattiest pork meat you can get your hands on and grind it finely yourself in the food processor or using a meat grinder.

Potato flour can be bought online or in most natural foods stores, as it is gaining popularity among people with gluten intolerance.

Ingredients

Serves 4 to 6

500 grams (~1 pound ground
   pork), at room temperature
1 1/2 teaspoon salt
250 milliliters (1 cup) milk,
   at room temperature
2 1/2 tablespoons potato flour
1/2 teaspoon freshly ground
   black pepper
1/4 teaspoon ground nutmeg
1/4 teaspoon powdered ginger
4 to 6 tablespoons butter
   for frying

Directions

Combine the pork, salt, and half the milk in a large bowl and stir until well combined. Stir in the potato flour, spices, and 1/2 cup of the remaining milk. Mix until well incorporated and the dough clumps together. If the mixture is dry, add the remaining 1/4 cup milk, one tablespoon at a time.

Form the dough into 5-centimeter/2-inch round patties. Place them on a plate and refrigerate for 30 minutes before cooking. Allow the patties to sit at room temperature for 10 minutes before frying.

Melt the butter in a frying pan over medium-high heat. Fry the patties for 5 to 6 minutes on each side. Be sure not to crowd the pan or the patties won't cook evenly or form a nice crust.

Norwegian Sauerkraut

Sauerkraut is eaten in all the Germanic countries, and Norway is no different. This recipe is one commonly used at Christmastime with both green and red cabbage.

If you make this recipe with red cabbage, mix the vinegar into the cabbage before warming, to help it stay a beautiful deep purple.

Ingredients

Serves 4 to 6

700 grams (1 1/2 pounds)
    cabbage, cored and shredded

2 apples, grated

1 teaspoon salt

2 teaspoons caraway seeds

250 milliliters (1 cup) water

2 teaspoons white vinegar

2 teaspoons sugar

Directions

In a large pot, simmer the cabbage, apples, salt, caraway seeds, and water for 45 minutes, stirring occasionally. Stir in the vinegar and sugar and cook for an additional 15 minutes, or until the cabbage is very soft but retains its shape. Serve and enjoy!

Pickled Herring

Pickled herring is eaten year-round but is most beloved at Christmastime.

Ingredients

Serves 4 to 6

5 medium sized salted herring
    fillets
500 milliliters (2 cups) milk
400 milliliters (1 2/3 cups) water
300 grams (1 1/2 cups) sugar
200 milliliters (3/4 cup) apple
    cider vinegar
1 tablespoon black peppercorns,
    whole
1 tablespoon allspice berries,
    whole
1 teaspoon ground cloves
1 tablespoon yellow mustard
    seeds
2 bay leaves
1 small red onion, thinly sliced
1 small knob of fresh ginger,
    thinly sliced

Directions

Soak the herring in a bowl of milk in the refrigerator for 24 hours. This will help draw the salt out of the fish.

Bring the water and sugar to a high simmer, allow to cool, then refrigerate overnight so the sugar water is ready when the fish has finished soaking.

Rinse the soaked herring with water and discard the milk. Cut the fish into 2 1/2-centimeter/1-inch strips.

Combine the chilled sugar water with the apple cider vinegar, pepper, allspice, cloves, mustard seeds, and bay leaves to make a brine. Set aside. Layer the herring, red onion, and ginger in a glass jar. Pour the brine over the herring and put on the lid. Refrigerate the herring for 24 hours before serving.

Pepperkake

If I had to use one word to sum up what Norwegian Christmas tastes like, that word would be *"pepperkake."* Pepperkake (literally "pepper cakes") are by far the most commonly eaten Christmas cookie in all of Norway. They usually appear in stores by early November and are eaten until the New Year. *Pepperkake* are served with coffee, tea, and especially *gløgg*, a spiced drink served warm, with or without alcohol.

In Norway, making homemade *pepperkake* is a welcomed event on most people's holiday calendar. This recipe can easily be doubled or used to make a *pepperkake hus*, or gingerbread house.

This *pepperkake* recipe calls for inverted sugar syrup (*lys sirup* in Norwegian), an ingredient uncommon in most U.S. kitchens but quite common in kitchens all over Europe. Buy inverted sugar syrup online via Amazon or in stores that sell European baking ingredients.

Ingredients

Makes 24 cookies

450 grams (3 cups) all-purpose
  flour
1 teaspoon baking powder
2 teaspoons ground cinnamon
1/2 teaspoon ground black
  pepper
1/2 teaspoon ground ginger
1/2 teaspoon ground cloves
150 grams (2/3 cup) butter
200 grams (3/4 cup) sugar
100 milliliters (1/3 cup) inverted
  sugar syrup (such as Lyle's
  Golden Syrup)
100 milliliters (1/3 cup) heavy
  cream

Directions

Sift together the flour, baking powder, cinnamon, pepper, ginger, and cloves into a large mixing bowl and set aside. In a medium saucepan, warm the butter, sugar, and sugar syrup over low heat and stir until the sugar dissolves, then stir in the cream. Add the sugar mixture to the flour mixture and stir to form a dough. Refrigerate the dough for at least 8 hours, or overnight.

Preheat the oven to 175° C/350° F. Line a baking sheet with parchment paper.

Remove the chilled dough from the refrigerator, place on a floured surface, and divide into four portions. Roll out one portion at a time very thin and cut with a cookie cutter.

Transfer the cookies to the baking sheet and bake for 10 to 12 minutes. When the cookies are light brown around the edges, they are done. Cool the cookies on a wire rack, then share, eat, and enjoy!

Krumkaker

The quintessential Norwegian Christmas cookie. Serve plain as a cone, or shaped as a bowl and filled with whipped cream and *multe* berries or jam. For this recipe, you will need a *krumkaker* iron and a cone shaper, both of which can be found from retailers online.

Ingredients

Makes 15 cookies

250 grams (1 1/4 cup) sugar
4 eggs
250 grams (1 cup) butter,
    melted
250 grams (1 cup) all-purpose
    flour
1 teaspoon ground cardamom

Directions

Whip eggs and sugar together until fluffy and pale yellow. Stir in the melted butter, flour, and cardamom. Mix until all ingredients are combined. Refrigerate the batter for 20 minutes.

Heat the *krumkaker* iron over medium-low heat. Pour a tablespoon of batter into the center of the hot *krumkaker* iron and bake until the batter is cooked and turns light golden brown. Use a cone shaper to form the *krumkaker* into cones while the cookie is warm. Alternatively, form the hot *krumkaker* into a bowl shape by molding it over the bottom of an upturned coffee mug.

Cool and enjoy plain, or fill with whipped cream and *multe* berries or your favorite jam. Store *krumkaker* in an air-tight container.

Sirupssnipper

Sirupssnipper are one of the traditional and classic cookie varieties one finds in Norway during *juletid* (the Christmas season). These cookies can be found in every supermarket in Norway beginning late November/early December. They are a delight to make at home, however, and fun to make with children. The recipe is very similar to *pepperkaker* in many ways, and the dough for both these cookies is prepared a day or two in advance. The secret to giving these cookies their signature color and snap is using dark inverted sugar syrup, also called "black treacle syrup" (*mørk sirup* in Norwegian).

Dark inverted syrup is a sister product to "golden" or light syrup and is very different in chemical make-up from molasses, corn syrup, honey, and basically every other liquid sweetener. It cannot be substituted for in this recipe, so you will need it to get your hands on it if you plan on baking these cookies. Buy your syrup on Amazon, or in a local store that sells European baking supplies.

Before measuring out the syrup, spray your measuring container with non-stick cooking spray or lightly coat with a neutral-flavored cooking oil. The syrup will slide right out when you pour it into the pot, and clean-up will be that much easier.

Ingredients

Makes 45 cookies

100 grams (3 1/2 ounces) dark
    inverted sugar syrup
60 grams (1/3 cup) sugar
50 milliliters (1/4 cup) heavy
    cream
60 grams (1/4 cup) butter
1 egg yolk
250 grams (2 cups) all-purpose
    flour
1/4 teaspoon ground ginger
1/2 teaspoon finely ground
    black pepper
1/2 teaspoon baking soda
100 grams (3 1/2 ounces) sliced
    blanched almonds

Directions

Melt the syrup, sugar, and cream together in a medium pot over medium-low heat. Add the butter and stir until it has melted. Cool the mixture until it is lukewarm, then stir in the egg yolk. Add the remaining ingredients and stir until well incorporated into the dough.

Remove the dough from the pan and knead gently on a lightly floured surface. Place the dough in a bowl, cover with plastic wrap/cling film, and refrigerate overnight or for at least 8 hours.

Preheat the oven to 180° C/350° F. Line a baking sheet with parchment paper and set aside.

Roll out the dough on a lightly floured surface until it is thin. (Be careful not to use too much flour!) Using a pastry wheel or knife, cut the dough into small diamond shapes about 3 3/4 centimeters/1 1/2 inches inch from long end to long end, then transfer to the baking sheet. Bake the cookies for 8 to 10 minutes, until light brown. Cool the cookies on a wire rack and store in an air-tight container.

Brunne pinner

Brune pinner, or "brown pins," are another classic and popular Norwegian cookie. I like *brune pinner* because they have a delicate, baked-in cinnamon flavor as well as a nutty texture thanks to the chopped almonds on top. This recipe calls for inverted sugar syrup and pearl sugar, both of which are common in many European countries but quite new to most American bakers.

While most bakers cut their *brune pinner* into diagonal strips when the cookies are still hot from the oven and just golden brown, I use a pizza cutter to cut mine into straight pins before they are baked. I also add a bit more color to my cookies by baking them 2 to 3 minutes longer than the traditional recipe suggests. Feel free to shorten the baking time by a few minutes if you like yours less brown and more golden, and to cut your cookies after baking if you fancy.

Ingredients

Makes 30 to 35 cookies

200 grams (3/4 cup plus
    2 tablespoons) butter
200 grams (1 cup) sugar
1 egg yolk
1 teaspoon inverted sugar syrup
1/2 teaspoon ground cinnamon
1 teaspoon vanilla sugar
1 teaspoon baking soda
300 grams (2 1/2 cups)
    all-purpose flour
1 egg, lightly beaten
Pearl or demerera sugar, for
    topping
Chopped almonds, for topping

Directions

Using a hand mixer or stand mixer, cream butter and sugar together well, then mix in the remaining ingredients. Place the dough on a lightly floured surface and knead lightly for about 1 minute. Divide into 4 portions and refrigerate for 15 minutes.

While the dough is chilling, preheat the oven to 175° C/345° F. Line a baking sheet with parchment paper and set aside. Thinly roll out one portion of the chilled dough on a lightly floured surface. Transfer the dough to the baking sheet and brush the dough lightly with the beaten egg, then sprinkle with the chopped almonds and pearl or demerara sugar. Bake for 10 to 12 minutes, or until the dough is lightly brown. Using a pizza cutter or a knife, cut the dough in strips.

Sandkaker

Sandkaker, literally "sand cookies," are very common in Norway during Christmastime and can be found at nearly all holiday parties.

Make sure you use *sandkaker* or tartlet tins to shape these cookies; they will turn out much prettier and look more traditional. If you don't have tartlet tins, a muffin tin can be used instead. Although most Norwegians grind their own almonds for these and all other Christmas cookies, I've used almond flour in this recipe with good results. These cookies can be served plain or topped with *multe* cream, a mixture of whipped cream and *multe* berries.

Ingredients

Makes 24 cookies

200 grams (3/4 cup plus 2
   tablespoons) butter
250 grams (2 cups) all-purpose
   flour
100 grams (1 cup) almond flour
1 egg
100 grams (1/2 cup) sugar

Directions

Using your hands or a pastry cutter, rub or cut the butter into the flour to form small, gravel-sized lumps. Add the almonds, egg, and sugar and mix until the mixture resembles sand. Refrigerate the dough for 1 hour.

Preheat the oven to 175° C/350° F. Remove the chilled dough from the refrigerator, section into 24 portions, and firmly press each section into *sandkaker* or tartlet tins. Transfer the tins to a baking sheet and bake in the middle rack of the oven for 12 to 15 minutes, or until lightly brown around the edges.

Remove the baking sheet from the oven and allow the cookies to cool for 7 to 10 minutes in the metal tins. Do not try to remove the cookies before they have cooled briefly, or they will fall apart. When the cookies have cooled slightly, gently remove them from the tins, then cool for an additional 20 minutes on a wire rack. Serve plain or topped with whipped cream and *multe* berries.

Hazelnut Macaroons

Norwegian hazelnut macaroons, or *nøttetopper,* are a great gluten-free alternative to serve this year at Christmastime. I love these little gems because they are made from staple pantry items and don't require any difficult-to-find ingredients.

Make sure you use raw, unroasted hazelnuts in this recipe—or for a slightly untraditional twist, use raw almonds instead.

Ingredients

Makes 24 cookies

3 egg whites

250 grams (~1 cup) raw hazelnuts, plus extra for decoration

200 grams (2 cups) powdered sugar

Directions

Preheat the oven to 180° C/350° F. Line a baking sheet with parchment paper and set aside.

Grind the hazelnuts in a food processor or blender. Whisk the egg whites until they form stiff peaks. Gently fold in the ground hazelnuts and sugar until just incorporated.

Using a tablespoon, drop lumps of the batter onto the baking tray. Gently press a hazelnut into the top of each cookie. Bake for 10 to 12 minutes.

Coconut Macaroons

Norwegian coconut macaroons, or *kokosmakroner,* are a popular, easy-to-prepare Norwegian Christmas cookie. I love this recipe because most of the ingredients are items I keep stocked in my pantry year-round, so whipping up a batch doesn't usually require an extra trip to the supermarket.

These cookies are gluten-free and delicious. Be sure to use unsweetened shredded coconut for these cookies so they don't turn out too sweet.

Ingredients

Makes 24 cookies

4 egg whites
250 grams (~1 cup) flaked,
    unsweetened coconut
150 grams (1 1/2 cups)
    powdered sugar
50 grams (3 1/2 tablespoons)
    vanilla sugar

Directions

Preheat the oven to 180° C/350° F. Line a baking sheet with parchment paper and set aside.

Whisk the egg whites until they form stiff peaks. Gently fold in the rest of the ingredients until just incorporated. Using a tablespoon, drop lumps of the egg white mixture onto a baking tray lined with parchment paper. Bake for 10 to 12 minutes.

Cloudberry Cream

Christmas just isn't Christmas without *multekrem* (cloudberry cream). Norwegians and other Scandinavians love *multe* berries, or cloudberries, for their tart flavor and unique texture. Cloudberries are high in minerals and antioxidants, which makes them perfect for sustaining your health in wintertime.

Fresh or even frozen cloudberries are extremely hard to find outside Scandinavia, so if you can get your hands on some you absolutely must make this dessert (and consider yourself extremely lucky!). If you live in Norway, substitute fresh cloudberries and 2 tablespoons of sugar for the jam listed below. Overall, this dessert is not overly sweet, and drizzling cloudberry liqueur on top of the finished dessert enhances the flavor.

Ingredients

Serves 6 to 8

*300 milliliters (1 1/4 cup)
    whipping cream*
*300 milliliters (1 1/4 cup)
    cloudberry jam*
Cloudberry liqueur (optional)

Directions

Whip the cream until soft peaks form. Gently fold the jam into the cream. Serve drizzled with cloudberry liqueur.

Norwegian Food Glossary

This glossary will help you navigate some of the most common foods in the Norwegian kitchen.

Blåbær: blueberries. Cultivated and wild varieties of this berry are available in supermarkets in larger cities. Highly prized and high in antioxidants.

Boller: buns. Literally translated as "balls," these sweet, cardamom-scented, yeasted buns are a staple in every bakery and cafe in Norway, as well as in most Norwegian households. They are much like British hot cross buns, but without the cross.

Brød: bread. Bread is eaten at breakfast and lunch, and as a snack or in-between meal throughout the day.

Brunost: brown cheese. *Brunost* is made from caramelized whey and comes in several varieties, with varying percentages of cow's and goat's milk blended together. The 100% goat's milk variety is called *geitost*, or "goat's cheese."

Bygg: barley. Served in muesli mixes and other grain products.

Fårikål: Norway's national dish, a homely one-pot stew containing cabbage, whole black peppercorns, and lamb.

Fenalår: dry-cured leg of lamb. Served particularly during Christmastime, but also year-round. *Fenalår* is paired with potato salad and *flatbrød* (flatbread), and often with aquavit, a grain spirit made with caraway seeds.

Flatbrød: flatbread. *Flatbrød* comes in many shapes but is always very thin and crispy. Made from wheat, barley, and rye, *flatbrød* accompanies soups, stews, cured meats, *rakfisk* (salted and fermented fish), and other savory dishes.

Havre: oats. Commonly eaten for breakfast—and not used in much else, so don't expect to find baked goodies like oatmeal cookies or oat and blueberry tarts in most bakeries. Nor will you find savory oatmeal in Norway. Quick-cooking and regular rolled oats are available in every store that sells food. Scottish oats, or steel-cut oats, are uncommon but oat groats can be found in nearly every health food store.

Kål: cabbage. Norwegians love cabbage, and many grocery stores and supermarkets are stocked with at least three varieties year-round. *Kål* (called white cabbage in most of the U.S.), *kinakål* (bok choy), *nykål* (new cabbage), and *savoykål* (savoy cabbage) are popular and common.

Kjøttkaker: meatballs, literally translated as "meat cakes." The Norwegian ones are closely related to their more popular Swedish cousins, but Norwegian meatballs are larger and flatter.

Klippfisk: bacalao, Norwegian dried and salted cod. Historically, this dried fish traded from Norway helped feed Europeans as far south as Spain and Portugal. It also fuelled trading between Norway and the rest of the world for centuries.

Knekkebrød: crispbread. A Danish or Swedish import but very common in Norway. *Knekkebrød* may resemble anything from sandpaper to a seeded cracker.

Komle: potato dumplings. *Komle* go by many regional names, including *klubber, raspeboller,* or simply *boller.*

Lefse: soft, pliable flatbread. *Lefse* are similar to Mexican tortillas and are served with butter, cinnamon and sugar, or *gomme* (a sweet spread) alongside coffee for an in-between meal. Also served wrap-style with *rakfisk*, potato, and raw onions during Easter in some parts of the country.

Matpakke: packed lunch. Literally translated as "food package," *matpakke* is a practical and beloved icon of Norwegian self-reliance and usually consists of two open-faced sandwiches topped with anything from brown cheese to liver pâté and pickles, wrapped in parchment paper to form a tidy package. The *matpakke* conjures up fond memories of school lunches and hiking trips with family for most Norwegians. Fruit and chopped vegetables like carrots may be served on the side.

In Norway, children take their own *matpakke* to school every day and receive a carton of milk from the school for lunch. Adults normally take their own *matpakke* to work, and eat their sandwich slices in the lunchroom, outside, or at their desks with their colleagues. *Matpakke* is so engrained in Norwegian society that (most) Norwegians tend to bring *matpakke* anytime they travel away from home for work or leisure.

Melk: milk. Sold in full-fat, light, and fat-free/skimmed forms. Fermented varieties such as kefir and *kulturmelk* are also commonly found.

Multe: cloudberries. Norwegians and other Scandinavians love cloudberries for their tart flavor and unique texture. Cloudberries are high in minerals and antioxidants, which makes them perfect for sustaining your health in wintertime. And Christmas just isn't Christmas without *multekrem* (cloudberry cream).

Pålegg: sandwich toppings. A general name given to deli-style sandwich fixings such as sliced cheeses, cold cuts, and sandwich spreads. Most Norwegian households have several varieties of *pålegg* on hand at all times.

Paprika: bell pepper (green, yellow, or red). In the U.S., most think of paprika as the powdered red pepper sprinkled over deviled eggs, but in Norway and most of Europe, it's the vegetable Americans know as bell pepper.

Pastinakk: parsnip. This vegetable is usually roasted in the U.K. and served with Sunday roast. In Norway you'll find it in stews, pureed, and roasted.

Pepperkake: spiced cookies. Literally "pepper cakes," these are by far the most commonly eaten Christmas cookie in all of Norway. Expect to see, smell, and hear people eating these crunchy treats every day during Christmastime.

Potet: potato. Quite likely the most commonly eaten vegetable in all of Norway, usually served as a boiled side dish with most meals. Several varieties are available in most stores.

Rabarbra: rhubarb. Grown in many Norwegian gardens in spring and rumored to be best before Midsummer, the longest day of the year, which falls in mid-June. Most Norwegians enjoy the stalks raw and dipped in sugar during the spring months.

Ruccula: rocket or arugula. This beloved peppery salad green is available in better-stocked markets.

Saft: currant juice concentrate. Historically, *saft* served as Norwegians' primary source of vitamin C and trace minerals during the long and dark winters.

Smør: butter. Made from whipping cream, or *fløte*. Some of the best butter in the world comes from Norway, and the best of the best by most accounts comes from the Røros region.

Torsk: cod. This plentiful white-fleshed fish is one of the enduring symbols of Norwegian cuisine. Commonly served poached, with butter and boiled potatoes.

Tyttebærsyltetøy: lingonberry jam. Lingonberries are cousins to the cranberry found in North America. This jam is served alongside meatballs and potatoes, with mushy peas and brown gravy.

Measurements

Norway (like most of the world) uses the metric system, which includes milliliters, grams, kilograms, etc. This differs from the U.S. customary system, which uses cups, ounces, pounds, pints, gallons, and so on. In this cookbook, recipes are presented in metric units, with U.S. customary units shown in parentheses.

Hard-to-Find Ingredients and Substitutions

A few ingredients are common to Norwegian cooking but hard to find outside of Norway. Sources for these ingredients are suggested here, and substitutions are noted where possible.

Almond paste

Almond paste is the less sweet, more textured cousin to marzipan. It can be hard to find outside of Scandinavia, but in most cases marzipan will make a decent substitute. When substituting in dessert recipes, be sure to use slightly less marzipan, as most traditional baked sweets and other desserts already include sugar in the dough.

Hjortetakksalt

This ingredient is still something of a mystery to me, but the name always makes me chuckle. Translated as "deer antler salt," it is called baking ammonia in the U.K. and is a forerunner to today's baking powder. *Hjortetakksalt* is very traditional in Norway and gives slightly more lift to baked goods than baking powder, but the quite distinctive smell can take some getting used to.

Inverted Sugar Syrup

Inverted sugar syrup is an ingredient uncommon in most U.S. kitchens, but quite commonly found in kitchens all over Europe. In Norway, inverted sugar syrup, or *lys/mørk sirup på norsk*, is used in several Christmas cookie recipes. Buy inverted sugar syrup online via Amazon or in stores that sell European baking ingredients.

Pearl Sugar

Pearl sugar is a very common ingredient in Norwegian baking and throughout the rest of Scandinavia. This type of sugar is typically used to top cookies, biscuits, and other sweet baked goods. It is a hard, coarse, white sugar that does not melt during baking, so it gives a very Scandinavian look to baked goods.

Pearl sugar is usually available from online sellers, but if not, substitute light demerara sugar or white caster sugar on top of cookies and pastries.

Potato Flour

As more and more people suffer from food allergies, naturally gluten-free potato flour is re-emerging as a reliable substitute for wheat flour in many dishes. In Norway it is often used for cakes, *flatbrød* (flatbread), and *fiskekaker* (fish cakes). Check your local health food store for potato flour, or order it online.

Vanilla Sugar

This is used in most Norwegian cookie and cake recipes. Back when vanilla was less readily available, burying a vanilla bean in a jar of sugar was a way to get as much flavor from the bean as possible over a long period of time. You can also soak your vanilla bean in a spirit like vodka or rum to make vanilla extract, a reliable substitute for vanilla sugar.

If you don't have vanilla sugar, try my recipe on thanksforthefood.com. My recipe is easy, although it takes a few months of curing to get the best results. Alternatively, you can use vanilla extract in most recipes; just substitute it teaspoon for teaspoon for vanilla sugar.

Yeast

Most traditional recipes for Norwegian baked goods require fresh yeast. As a more budget-friendly option, active dry yeast can often be used as a substitute, although the resulting taste will be less "yeasty" and the texture of the raw dough will at first be wetter.

Index